BESIDE MY SELF

D1826457

BESIDE MY SELF
The Memoirs of a China Cabinet

Publisher imprint: Australian Lesbian and Gay Archives (ALGA)

ALGA is the biggest repository of historical materials about
LGBTIQ experience in Australia. The Archives was established
in 1978. It is a volunteer, community-based organisation.

ISBN 978-0-6488591-0-9 (paperback)
ISBN 978-0-6488591-1-6 (epub)
ISBN 978-0-6488591-2-3 (hardback)

A catalogue record for this book is available from the National
Library of Australia.

Images. Thanks to Richard Riley for Michael on Horseback 1978,
Paul Harris for Michael in Northcote 2020 and Mazz Image
for Michael and Paul van Reyk 1996. Every effort was made to
identify the other unknown photographers.

I thank the following for copyright permissions: Pam Brown for
permission to quote from her poems ' 'Ol' Shallow Throat' and
'West End Blues'; Andrea Goldsmith for permission to quote
from Dorothy Porter's poem 'Faith'; Mick Forbes for permission
to quote from John Forbes' poem 'Watching the Treasurer'; and
Gary Dunne, co- executor with Gavin Harris, for permission to
quote from Ian MacNeill's poem 'Amelia Earhart'.

Every effort has been made to trace copyright holders and we
apologise in advance for any unintentional omission. We would
be pleased to insert the appropriate acknowledgement in any
subsequent edition.

Design Management: Leigh Raymond
Book Design: Stuart Geddes
Printed in Australia by: IngramSpark

A note on the type: There's a typographic tension at play in this
book, between symmetrical and asymmetrical composition – a
key debate in modernist graphic design – played out here with
two contemporary re-imaginings of typographic workhorses –
Tiempos Text (Klim) and Field Grot (Matter of Sorts).

BESIDE MY SELF
The Memoirs of a China Cabinet
Michael Hurley

Australian Lesbian and Gay Archives

For
Moira Carmody (1953–2020)
Liz Jacka and Kevin Mead

This memoir fans out like a peacock's tail.
Eye spots on the splayed feathers stare
and the topknots on stems
remind me of Brunswick Street Fitzroy.

I

I am polishing the outside of my silver teapot. It shines beautifully when finished. The elegance of its shape made evident again, it sits complete, contained, an object of beauty. It gives me pleasure. I suspect that makes me, formally at least, an aesthete, if not homosexual, and possibly bourgeois to boot.

It is the proportionate form of the teapot that captivates me. It is slung low rather than stretched high. It is simple in all regards (the spout, the hinged lid, the slightly plumped elliptical body) but one, the handle, a mix of curves, flourishes and air holes. The handle is a conceit, a bit of mischief, carefully crafted with resting places for the thumb and little finger, both crucial for the pouring of the tea: modernism with a backward flounce that registers other more ornate times.

On the base, it is stamped Perfect Teapot followed by a list of worldwide patents. A little research tells me that Perfect Teapots were produced by the Robur Tea Company and are made of electroplated nickel silver. Patented in 1927, they were popular in Australia for most of the twentieth century.

The teapot I have come to realise is complete as a single object, but in another way not entirely so. Other teapots of the same Perfect kind are accompanied by a metal mesh tea infuser that contains the tea leaves and hangs inside from the rim just below the lid. Jack Wallace tells me the infuser too has a handle. Mine is missing its infuser.

My pleasure in the silver teapot remains. I consider bringing out the blue china tea set for six people that Kevin Mead gave me in about 1980 to sit with it, but that has its own teapot and the glass cabinet from IKEA is already full. A Meissen cup and saucer sit on the top shelf, a gift from my friends Leigh Raymond and Winston Appleyard after they went to Germany in 2016. Beside it is a three-piece set: Susie Cooper's 'Recumbent Deer' cup, saucer and plate from the Wedgwood Women Designers of the 20th Century series. Mitch Cleary gave that to me, for my fiftieth birthday in 1999. Next shelf down is the silver teapot. Beside it is a Bauhaus designed, Alessi produced, stainless steel ashtray from my visit to the Bauhaus Archive in Berlin, also in 2016. The designer was Marianne Brandt, the only woman to have worked in the *Metallwerkstatt* of the Bauhaus. I had coveted the ashtray on a previous visit, but baulked at the price, despite Graham Willett's urgings to buy it. The second time, and with the encouragement of my friend Marshall Feldman from LA, I breathed deep and bought it. In front of the teapot and to the side of the ashtray lies a keyring. On it is a metal cast bar, sandblasted for a flat matte finish. It spells out 'desire' in capital letters. Leigh also gave me that. It comes from the Museum of Old and New Art in Hobart.

The glazed blue landscape and white background pattern on the out-of-view china tea set is reminiscent in colouring and imagery of the Willow pattern used by English ceramicists at the end of the eighteenth century and after. They had copied it ('imported', 'inspired by') from the Chinese, possibly from exported pieces produced in what was then known by English speakers as Canton, now Guangzhou. The pattern on my pieces is, however, firmly English. There is a rustic country house with trees, but no willows or pagodas or the pairs of birds favoured in the Chinese original. Physically, the china is a little thick, not quite fine. Some months ago, I discussed with Kevin the absence of markings on the base of any of the tea set items. He speculated that the set might be an unacknowledged, Chinese mass-produced 'take' from the 1970s of the earlier English willow pattern design. Imperial simulations re-circulate, in part as un-historicised nostalgia. A serene idealised version of the way things used to be is frozen in another time courtesy of international trade. An imagined what was, still is. The china sits on shop shelves, quietly 'tasteful' rather than fashionable.

After I moved from Sydney to Melbourne for the first time, in the mid-seventies, I realised a year or so later that I had to make a determined effort to maintain contact with Sydney friends. I did. I made sure I kept visiting Sydney. Kevin visited me in Melbourne several times as did Moira Carmody. Kevin came originally from Kurri Kurri in the Hunter Valley. Kurri was known for its coal fields, still is by many, then its aluminium smelter, and now the wineries of the wider valley. Moira was a British immigrant as a child. So was I. Not that you can tell from how we speak.

On one of those trips to Melbourne Kevin bought me the tea set. On another of his visits we went to northern Victoria to visit Peter Crowley who was teaching at Wodonga High. We fished together from a dinghy on the Hume Weir, gently bobbing in the shadows of late afternoon and the blanched company of long dead trees left there years after the weir wall extension increased the area submerged by stored water. Almost forty years later, if I shut my eyes, I can still see the light on the weir's surface and hear the water lapping on the side of the dinghy. Somewhere under the extended lake is 'Old' Tallangatta. On the Victorian side of the wall was Bonegilla migrant camp. If you followed the Murray Valley Highway you came to the Bandiana army camp and then Wodonga.

My china cabinet sits in a small TV lounge in the middle of a single-fronted, weatherboard house in the inner north of Melbourne. The hall runs through one side of the room. In another age, it might have been called a parlour, but that would be pushing it now. A parlour was traditionally a public space within the house that kept the rest of the house private. It was a place for visitors. Propriety – a mix of respectability, virtue, courtesy and civility – required it. This changed, to a degree, when open plan architecture replaced smaller rooms with larger spaces, more window area and more daylight. Walls came down, casual socialising sprawled, but chipped china remained iffy. Heating and cooling bills went up.

To the left of my front gate on entry is a leggy 'Moonlight' grevillea that blooms creamy white brushes. The bees love it, as do the wattle birds, and me too. It was a gift from Rose Flynn and Mitch Cleary soon after moving in.

In his book *Queer Domesticities. Homosexuality and Home Life in Twentieth-Century London*, cultural historian Matt Cook suggests that various emerging domestic flourishes were early twentieth century markers of queer difference which in the second part of the century became 'a trenchant stereotype.' We need not take that negatively. Cook was simply pointing out as others have done that stereotyping is one way that aspects of queer and other cultures are 'typified' in a process that allows public recognition, vigorous discussion and ongoing negotiation of how 'we' want to be represented by ourselves and others. Richard Dyer, now an emeritus professor in film studies, argued in *Gays and Film* (1977) that one key aspect of stereotyping is who controls it and to what end. There is no assumption on Cook's, Dyer's or my part that we all want the same thing.

Visual art and popular culture have a habit of disrupting propriety, both domestically and publicly. Robert Mapplethorpe's 1980 photo that we know as 'Man in a Polyester Suit' is one good example. It doubles as a headless portrait and penile coronal display. Whoever thought polyester and penile skin could be so adroitly colour matched, or imagined a penis might be vertically aligned with the buttons on a waistcoat? Shortly after Mapplethorpe died in 1989 US senator Jesse Helms used a Mapplethorpe retrospective to try and change the nature and extent of national obscenity laws. Homosexuality and AIDS were collapsed into each other in a very public vitriolic attack.

A second example involves me seeing the work of fashion photographer Herb Ritts in gay men's lounge rooms, hallways, bedrooms. Large posters of 'Fred with Tires' (1984) asserted male musculature. It was in the eighties in Sydney, but it might have been in any big city attuned to what was happening in the USA. Fred was muscled, with shiny biceps, pecs, abs, greased and greasy, body twisted to face front with a large vehicle tyre in each hand, in work overalls that dropped to his waist and were held by a wide leather belt. He stood in an industrial workspace, glorious in dirt. A young man in his prime. Piles of tyres to the viewer's right, he and the detritus standing on a concrete floor. Ritts disrupted any notion of gay masculinity as a matter only of effete charm. Trenchant yes, head-turning, yet not necessarily opposed to a nice bit of china. Posters and porcelain. They often came together in lounge rooms.

The china in my cabinet, or as much of it as fits, a metre or so from the television, might be said to be in its proper place. It is visible but protected from the casual wear and tear of everyday use. I put it out to remind myself of it, and to enjoy seeing it, though that does not seem to have increased its use other than for special occasions. Indeed, I would not dream of using the Bauhaus Alessi ashtray. It is as simple as not wanting to tarnish

7

the pristine surface as though to do so would be to spoil it. I recall how surprised I was when I first held it. Its feathery lightness belied how it looked. I had expected weight. A year or two back, I moved the cabinet into the lounge from the adjacent open plan living area, where it had displayed Buddhas, a Ganesh, a souvenir of the Taj Mahal from Anil, bits of ephemeral art, some kitsch, several snowdomes. I also like each of them, but I am in a de-cluttering phase. For the moment they sit in a box.

Neatness, however satisfying, is no guarantee of serenity. Nor is propriety.

In David Lean's 1945 film *Brief Encounter*, Laura, a married woman in the suburbs of London, meets a stranger, and tentatively, yet progressively, acquaints herself with the dangers of 'forbidden love'. In the end, circumstances ensure she behaves 'well'. It is a melodramatic narrative of coming undone, and conflicted female restraint bought about by the necessities of marriage, child-rearing and conformity. As the film closes, Laura is sitting in an armchair being embraced by and tearfully embracing her husband Fred who has just thanked her for coming back to him. An ordinary enough tale still, its associated distresses resonate with a variety of audiences. It is also a 'steamy' romance that pulses with gloriously powerful black and white shots of coal fired, steam locomotives arriving and departing. Steamy timing punctuates the film, declaring the arrhythmic spaces between domesticity, the wider world, personal desire and shame. It is a female centred, heterosexual, very 'British' film, and is often very funny in its excessiveness.

On its re-release seventy years later, John Patterson, a *Guardian* reviewer, wrote of the film having a 'displaced hysteria' that 'finally infects the audience's mind [and] makes *Brief Encounter* a rollercoaster of social and emotional horrors.'

After the film's original release, many homosexual men also began to see it as emblematic of their story. Dyer suggested in his 1993 book *Brief Encounter* that they identified with the film because of how it handled 'powerfully emotional material' – 'forbidden love'. Fear of being found out results in a retreat into respectability. Laura's home, he says, is her closet.

It is nearly thirty-five years since Richard wrote about the film, and there are as he later noted multiple gay male cultures, not just one, but the comment still holds for many viewers now even within a diversity of homosexual desires. We all engage in 'identification', irrespective of our identities. We identify with various modes of feeling, situations, evocations. Otherwise the film would be unwatchable for many. No doubt for some it is. Nor does everyone like black and white films. Laura is made abject by her straying emotions. They take her away from home and hearth, threaten good order. She is on the edge of chaos, horrified yet tantalised, tormented, smoked out by what she wants to explore. (The entire affair occurs in time snatched during routine shopping trips.) Decorum falls like underpants after the elastic fails.

Laura's voiceover: *It's awfully easy to lie when you know that you're trusted implicitly. So very easy, and so very degrading.*

There is more than integrity, guilt and respectability at stake. We have entered a maelstrom of emotion.

Circumstance, however, draws Laura back from the edge – 'he' announces he is going to Africa. The first time I saw that scene, I wanted to laugh at the plot, probably did, such a cheap out – but even so I was right there with her. So was the British empire – 'Africa.' I laugh again at the melodrama and identify simultaneously with the romantic desperation.

I also think of Doris Day's 1953 hit 'Secret Love'. George Michael did a big band version in December 1999, saluting the sounds of the twentieth century. Desperation has moved to impatience. There's nothing to be hidden, no more secrets. Doris was singing of the first flush of romance before the subject of her love is informed and she can tell the (American) world. George was singing of a change in social and personal circumstances that made possible a public declaration of his gay identity. A year earlier he had been arrested for a 'lewd act' in Beverley Hills.

Ongoing disorderly contact threatens the neatness of lounge rooms. As seen in *Brief Encounter*, it involved unspoken, potentially deceitful sexual interactions, outside of the marriage and the home. Such acts and their implications are barely thinkable, much less speakable, yet Laura teeters on the edge. In the railway café, flirtations between members of the working-class staff also mark out the ambiguities of what is acceptable and what is not in a music hall burlesque of propriety. What Laura can't accept is that she also wants things to be otherwise, at least momentarily.

Brief Encounter dramatises the possibility of sex and love elsewhere. (In this version the two go hand in hand.) The emotional shock of this possibility is what Laura recognises, but not the possibility that she can act. Her husband Fred's thanks, however, suggest he intuits how far she went towards going 'away', how close she came. That's the territory, no-no land and its allure. Over time, the audiences for *Brief Encounter* grew, and its reception became ever more contemporary. In the age of websites like ashleymadison.com that offer the opportunity of clandestine affairs to married heterosexuals, Tinder for dating and the gay/bi/trans phone apps, *Brief Encounter* might seem quaint, but it is not. The emotional terrain it covers remains commonplace as does divorce. What any cursory exposure to the apps makes evident are the public and private compromises embedded in the marriage apparatus. People make do. This is the mainstream. It has its challenges. I am with British playwright and novelist Neil Bartlett on these matters. In 1996 he said in an interview with cultural theorist Alan Sinfield,

> my mainstream is very picky; one that most people wouldn't recognise. It is deeply queer, kinky, complicated, melodramatic, over-determined, disruptive and disrupted.

Restraint as any practitioner of the finer erotic arts knows is productive, but there are disciplinary differences between fine-tuning corporeal delight, managing the proprieties of yearning and conforming to mainstream social norms. The latter requires ever closer attention to duty, whether that is thought about in religious, secular or political terms. One result of this is that melodrama becomes both commonplace and complicated.

Propriety leaks, especially where desire is concerned. (I am not referring to the genteel holding of a handkerchief to a runny nose to dry the run, though I could.) Think of the seepages that occur as you cut into a perfectly poached egg. Sealed egg white gives way to warm, runny yolk. It permeates its surrounds. Perhaps that's why some prefer the soft-boiled egg. Contained by the cooked egg-white, the shell and the egg cup, it requires a deft, neat beheading, followed by scooping,

lifting, drip-free swallowing. Not everything
can be instantly explained by class and imperial
power. We can celebrate Ena Sharple's feistiness
in *Coronation Street* as much as we like and adore
the hair net that in a sense metaphorically keeps
the coat broaches in place, but it is her tough
moralistic respectability that gave and gives me the
horrors. Yet it too makes me laugh even as I groan.
Things overlap. There was not much room for
unauthorised sexual pleasures or gay manoeuvre in
the snug of the Rover's Return. Even the peas being
shelled over a milk stout rarely fell to the floor.
Social acceptance is the reward for self-disciplined
conformity to convention. Forbidden love is forced
to hover. It is there and not there, visible and not
visible. Rigidity produces hysteria, anger, violence,
shame, or in the case of sloppy gobbling, disgust. I
said gobbling, not gobbing.

All this, and the love of a porcelain cup, but
where is the difference? Sometimes there is none.
Other times it is so marked as to be unthinkable.
Oscar Wilde: 'I find it harder and harder every day
to live up to my blue china.' Oscar's remark referred
to two large blue vases, rather than cups. Richard
Ellmann in his biography of Wilde suggests the
vases were possibly Sèvres. Porcelain aesthetes
are determinedly and systematically frivolous
when faced with Scottish Calvinism, Wesleyan
Methodism, puritan politics and social propriety.

That snug the past, where some things sit fug
warm.

The Susie Cooper set that Mitch gave me
was issued by Wedgwood in 1997 in a 'limited'
run of 5000 to mark the coming millennium. The
design is one of Cooper's last for Wedgwood and
had not been previously issued. Its colourings are
relatively muted, except for the high-finish glaze.
The overall effect is again stylised elegance. The

deer shapes are fluid, 'artistic'. I consult Marshall in LA via WhatsApp on the design. I ask if it is 'retro' arts and craft. He puts it as transitional between Art Nouveau and Art Deco. When, in return, I suggest retro early modernist, he says that is a good description. I am pleased. It covers our uncertainties. (Later: I now suspect the design may have been done in the 1960s.) I ring Mitch and ask how she knew Cooper's work. She speaks of her time in London in the late eighties and early nineties and of coming across Cooper's and Clarice Cliff's work in London markets – 'pricey even then'. She recalls a now long-gone arcade in Hawthorn, Melbourne, near where she worked at Swinburne Institute (1982–1984). In the arcade was an antiques shop: 'one day I fell in love with a cup.'

Mitch bought the cup. At my request, she sends me a photo to jog my memory. The cup is art deco fine china. It has a sharply angled, triangular handle; the green upper area of the cup's body is undercut by a slanted black and silver sloping band with white underneath to the base. There is no sign of chintz. Mitch likes a straight line and a curve. She taught Maths.

The design of the cup demands the browsing buyer move on from conventional flowery prettiness in reassuring shapes. This is lip-to-base angular cool, in shape and colouring. That said, there is far more to deco china than geometric angularity versus degrees of floral decoration. Clarice Cliff moved back and forth between them with ease, playing with colour, shape and abstraction. At the time that Mitch bought me the Cooper set, she bought herself a Clarice Cliff cup, saucer and plate from the same Wedgwood series. The colouring is hotter – orange, red, yellow and black encircle a house with chimney, trees and hills. White space cools the effects, balances them out.

13

Cooper's design was arguably safer. 'Elegance' too has class connotations: 'tastefully refined' through deliberate cultivation.

Mitch and I first met at a party in 1977. Well that is what my memory says, though Mitch thinks we may have met earlier. In my memory we were in someone's upstairs lounge in a Clifton Hill or North Fitzroy terrace, talking at the doorway to the balcony as others danced in dim light on a bare board floor. I was somewhat shy however Mitch had and has an easy manner, a presence. I relaxed enough to enter the conversation. I wonder who introduced us. I was still relatively new to Melbourne. Maybe she simply began speaking with me without introduction, as one did at parties. In the months following we did a couple of gigs speaking about homosexuality and gay liberation to student groups in Ballarat and at what is now RMIT university. It was Mitch who fifteen years after we met put me on to the Louisiana crime novels of James Lee Bourke that kept me awake long into the night in her house in Fitzroy off Brunswick Street. Ten years after that we went together to hear John le Carré speak on his novel *The Constant Gardener* and the perfidies of pharmaceutical companies in the African AIDS epidemic. Small things are as much the stuff of constancy as bigger ones. Thirty years after that first meeting it was to her I turned when after a long period of looking I at last found a house to buy. Mitch is a canny bidder at auctions and her nerve is stronger than mine. I live in that house.

Aestheticism was not high on our agendas then, and I am not sure Mitch would say it is for her now. We both had some sense of what we found interesting and who we liked and were open to learning new things. I knew very little of Wilde at the time we met, but the various personalities in the

Bloomsbury Group – Virginia Woolf, Vita Sackville-West, Lytton Strachey, Duncan Grant etc – were often talked of. As they were with Moira too, mostly on the phone.

English aestheticism had its motivational origins in the failures of mid-nineteenth-century Christianity. Anglicanism had collapsed into a mix of High Church bells and smells, Broad-Church liberalism and Evangelical rigidity. Many adopted the Methodist alternative, some departed for Rome (the 'Oxford Movement') and others to ancient Greece (Walter Pater, Oscar Wilde).

Early in that century-long process of Anglican disaggregation, William Wilberforce had become both an evangelical and an anti-slavery activist. Evangelicals then were frowned on socially and politically, and slavery was vigorously defended by the mercantile establishment. For Wilberforce religion involved the implantation of a vigorous principle in one's heart. It was a strict sect version of the relation between the conscience, self-regulation and god that insisted one must also do good.

In place of religion, Wilde positions fine china as a metonym for all that is beautiful. Jane Austen would have been mortified. There is no inner guide in Oscar's frivolity towards good behaviour – no active principle. It is replaced by the standards and forms of beautiful objects. Their artificiality demands attention, incites desire and delivers sensual pleasure. Wilde is mischievously sincere and philosophically rooted in aestheticism. I see resistance through parody. It is an invitation to disorderly living. A minority sexual sensibility is in play. Not living up to his blue china might be heard as a confession, both meant as such and not. He says in the essay 'The Decay of Lying' (1889) that 'Lying, the telling of beautiful untrue things, is the proper aim of Art.'

Or as others said one way or another at the time, it's those bloody novels that corrupt.

For my purposes here, aestheticism and decadence are roughly synonymous. Decadence was and is a minority persuasion that sits well to the side of regulations ensuring the lineage of inheritance and ordered domestic economies.

> When you do become engaged to someone, I, or your father, should his health permit him, will inform you of the fact. An engagement should come on a young girl as a surprise, pleasant or unpleasant, as the case may be. It is hardly a matter that she could be allowed to arrange for herself.
> (Lady Bracknell in Wilde's *The Importance of Being Earnest*, 1895)

Earnestness mocked elicits delight. The audience groans. Duty trumps pleasure. The audience laughs. Light heartedness is sinful. Desire disrupts. Where is proportion here? Delight returns. It was never gone, just rearranged. Put away in a cupboard.

As the English social theorist Jonathan Dollimore points out in his discussions of perversity, order and disorder are as much next to each other as opposites. The threat of disorder not so much draws ever nearer, it is always already there, lurking, beckoning, seducing, demanding attention. Hence Ena Sharple's moralism: sensual desire must be nipped in the bud before it flowers. It is very unlikely she would order a cocktail, but I entertain myself by imagining her demanding 'a clitoral orgasm and a bag of chips'.

However, decadence is also often associated with the aristocracy and the *haute bourgeoisie*. They are seen as overly indulgent and socially parasitic. In Bertolucci's film *1900*, for example, the drug taking, urbane, homosexual uncle introduces his land-owning nephew to 'sophistication', the world of fine art and partying. The *haute bourgeois* in this narrative are often corruptors. Excess is aristocratic degeneracy, and experimental male sex in adolescence is a passing phase. Ironically these views were also evident in the morality of various communist parties. Or as Jamaican-born British sociologist Stuart Hall put it in 'The Hard Road to Renewal' (1988),

> The truth is that traditionalist ideas, the ideas of social and moral respectability, have penetrated so deep inside socialist consciousness that it is quite common to find people committed to a radical political programme underpinned by wholly traditional feelings and sentiments.

That said, *1900* is one of my many favourite films, largely because of its historical sweep. It is an anti-fascist epic, a class saga, a family drama, a sexual romp, all seasoned with vignettes of murderous brutality. Take your pick. The cinematography and the Verdi score are glorious I have been totally absorbed every time, bouncing from one acutely realised vignette to the next, putting the pieces together. Fifty years pass in four hours seven minutes or six hours if you watch the Director's cut.

The moment Wilde was arrested on a charge of public indecency on April 6, 1895, ticket sales at the box office for *The Importance of Being Earnest* collapsed. His name was removed from the programme and the advertising. The play closed on May 8.

Brief Encounter came at a very precise end-of-war moment. Looser sexual and emotional mores that ran riot during the war were tightening rapidly. The explorations made possible by disordered delirium were reined in. The utility ware china that emerged in the late 1930s in the USA ('Knowles') had become simpler in Britain when war regulations required plain white pottery. Decoration was simplified, if not bypassed. All resources went to the war. Good china went hand in hand with social constraint, even if the hand may have shaken when the tea was poured, only to sit there, forgotten, the would-be drinker oblivious, deaf to a kind husband.

The freedom gained by many working-class women was lost the moment the men came home from war and were given their jobs back. The middle class had a job to do and many working-class families aspired to respectability if not gentility. The detachable white collar of the middle-class male that made starching easier for the stay at home wife was getting less common, but there were nappies to consider – for whitening, not starching. Divorce and infidelity were largely still unthinkable for women with children. None of this is so surprising when the world had been turned upside down. People wanted a secure 'normality' often practiced through a combination of outwardly refined domesticity and drawn curtains.

Two years after *Brief Encounter*, India and Pakistan gained independence. Caribbean immigrants began arriving in Britain in 1948. They had served the 'mother country' in two world wars. The empire came 'home' to roost, even as British emigration took off again. Many went to 'White Australia', my parents and I included. That was 1952. I was two.

The problem in those post-war social circumstances, as they played out in *Brief Encounter,* is not so much that the choice of person is often out of kilter with what is needed to sustain a life of manageable erotic disorder, as it is the lack of social value given to social forms that enable and support it – open relationships, polyamory, the kindness of strangers. Instead, what the dominant moral order requires is public conformity and private deceit, the territory otherwise known as that of the double standard. Much like the kitchen cupboards, it is built-in.

I'm with Peggy Lee. Is that all there is?

Marriages began in dance halls, as did babies. Well, outside and down the nearby, unlit lane. I hear Peggy Lee with pleasure. Others sang it before her and many more after, but the style of her version has been linked to that of Kurt Weill's 'Alabama Song' and 'Surabaya Johnny'. Dancing is expansively social, and sometimes defiantly licentious.

My manicurist Nicole is organising the cake for the wedding of two of her gay male friends. The event is being held in a rooftop bar with room to dance. One hundred are going. The cake maker advises she order a cake that will serve only eighty of the guests. The rest won't want any. We discuss the palaver and stress weddings can involve. Nicole's line is direct: 'It's a wedding, not the marriage.' She looks forward to the dancing.

My own dancing began in about 1965 when the local Anglican minister in Bandiana started a monthly dance where we learned to both waltz and jive. The dance nights stopped abruptly when someone put Normie Rowe's 1965 hit 'It Aint Necessarily So' on the turntable – 'The things that you're liable to read in the bible, aint ...' The record player was turned off halfway through the track. Cultures collided. We continued at occasional school dances, in garages and in back yards at teenage birthday parties before we graduated to lounge rooms. It was only when I joined Gay Liberation in 1972 that my dancing took off again: the parties at Camp NSW in Balmain, the Roundhouse at the University of NSW, Sydney University Union, Paddington and Glebe Town Halls, private parties, bars, national homosexual conferences, Mardi Gras, the Sleaze Ball, cattle sheds, warehouse parties in Alexandria and a shearing shed outside Wagga.

Brief Encounter was scripted by Noel Coward from his 1936 short play, *Still Lives*. The play takes place over a year. The film's version of the time frame seems in my memory much shorter, 'briefer'. The brief encounters hinted at by the film title, wartime shenanigans, couldn't continue with quite the same abandon when transferred into suburban heterosexuality. Yet there were remainders and reminders of gay life from before the play, and before the film. John Lehmann's 1976 novel *In the Purely Pagan Sense* is as good as any place to start if you want to explore this further.

Coward did a quite specific theatrical version of gay in the 1920s, and after. His image became his signature: the silk, polka dot dressing gown, the elongated cigarette holder, the drawled 'darling'. Social aspiration, taste and a degree of performative daring went hand in hand. Some Oxford undergraduates of the time like the character Anthony Blanche in Evelyn Waugh's *Brideshead Revisited* (1945) took associated liberties, as had Waugh himself. Class gave a degree of protection to particular forms of overt homosexuality, though rugby-club hearties were a threat. Waugh was bothered by what he saw as the cultural confusions and social wildness of the twenties which he satirised in *Decline and Fall* (1928). He later converted to Catholicism. Philip Core speaks of Somerset Maugham, Cecil Beaton, Ivor Novello and Coward as representing a form of camp adored by the English upper classes: 'an outrageous but unprosecutable *arbiter elegantarium*.'

'Unprosecutable', I wonder. Exclusion and discrimination come to mind, as does disdain.

Radclyffe Hall's novel *The Well of Loneliness* which asked for the right to existence for sexual 'inverts', in this case lesbians, was banned shortly after publication in 1928. It contained the sentence 'That night they were not divided.' Gasp. David Smith in the *Guardian* reports one doctor at the time referred to lesbianism as 'a danger to the well-being of a nation' and the novel was not released in Britain until 1949, the year I was born.

Many of us were delighted much later still by Coward's outrageousness, though not always comfortable with how it threatened other kinds of masculinity. Coward had trouble with class. One had to be artistically proper. Go figure. He did.

Others, like George Orwell, understood class differently. His *Down and Out in Paris and London* was published in 1933 and *The Road to Wigan Pier* in 1937. Both are personal journalistic investigations of poverty. Orwell recognised pleasure and the delights of vulgarity, but he was more than a bit prim about them.

It is Orwell's insistent old-fashioned masculinity I have my eye on. Orwell was not homosexual. He did not need to find public speaking positions or ways of being that allowed for or created a degree of homosexual legitimacy, even though he knew several homosexual men personally. Mostly when he spoke of homosexuality, he sneered at 'fashionable pansies', 'the pansy left' and the 'nancy poets' – 'pious sodomites' all. Stephen Spender at whom Orwell directed the 'nancy poet' gibe, was kinder than I am being. His biographer Gordon Bowker says Spender attributed Orwell's intermittent 'homophobic outbursts' to his rebellion against the public school. Whatever its origins, Orwell scholar Ben Clarke suggests, it was nasty and arguably more than occasional.

Aside: Spender's daughter from his second marriage is married to Barry Humphries. Spender was friends with the poet W.H. Auden and novelist Christopher Isherwood and spent time with them in Berlin. Some people live on edges, cross borders (with or without papers) leave and return.

Orwell was simultaneously an anti-authoritarian and a moralist. By itself, anti-authoritarianism can be articulated with conservative politics. He simply saw socialism as a removal of the worst socio-economic abuses but set alongside an ongoing present consisting of 'the family, the pub, football and local politics.' The former was a matter of justice. The latter was social conservatism. He opposed birth control, homosexuality, and feminism, and encouraged having large families. Keep the men socially illiterate and the women pregnant.

The journalist A.N. Wilson said in a review of Robert Colls' biography of Orwell that,

> He disliked religion, but his ideal England was populated by old maids cycling to communion in the autumn mist, and he decreed that his funeral should follow the Prayer Book service.

That Orwell favoured the idyllic in his personal values is not that surprising. Nasty times are made bearable, given solace, by familiar patterns of order. They console. China cabinets included. My parents retired to Perth in the mid-seventies for my father's health. Visiting some years later, I was surprised to see two gold ringed Constable reproduction plates on the loungeroom wall. I recall no wall decorations in the homes I grew up in other than calendars, but maybe I was not looking properly. The plates are of classic Constable pictures, 'The Cornfield' and 'Salisbury Cathedral', made in Staffordshire by the Lord Nelson Pottery.

Cultural sensibilities take time to emerge, mine certainly have, as does at least a provisional sense that in some ways one has managed to 'make it' in life. That comment is me projecting onto my parents. The plates are not currently on my walls.

My problem with Orwell is not with his tastes. It is with his demand that we accept his version of masculinity rule at the expense of others: women, homosexuals, heterosexual men who do things differently like, to jump a few decades, British artist Grayson Perry. God knows what Orwell made of drag, cross-dressing, transsexuals.

Where, I found myself asking, both during the writing of the paragraphs above and sometime later, has this hostility to Orwell come from? After all, I would still recommend *Homage to Catalonia*, *Animal Farm* and *1984* amongst others on a list of books that anyone might consider reading. I think the answer lies in the shadow of shame. I know that voice of Orwell's. It activates memories of gender shaming. I was probably about four and playing dress-ups in the shed and was told to take off whatever I had donned, perhaps cast-offs of my mother's. I was made to know I had crossed a line simply by a tone and a look. I had done wrong. That tone and that look have a social lineage and an aesthetic consequence. It is a line that marks out what is acceptable clothing for males and is in that sense an intervention of a conservative kind. It is also psychosocial. That boy of four, me, knew that intuitively. One must not enjoy delight. To do so is shameful.

I wasn't meaning to dismiss Coward, when I made the remark about class, but to draw attention to the tensions and complications of being publicly 'out' at different times in the first seventy years of the twentieth century. Success, as in the case of Coward, often required a stylised theatrical conformity, though some resisted at a cost, mostly on the street rather than in theatres and drawing rooms. By on the street I do not mean homosexual political demonstrations. Quentin Crisp's autobiography *The Naked Civil Servant* (1968) comes to mind as does Jack Gold's 1975 film version of it. We were riveted by it the night it was shown on tv. Crisp came out in 1931 and his public encounters in the thirties were often potentially, or actually violent incidents, elsewhere spoken of as 'unsavoury' involving as they did henna hair dye, nude modelling, street cruising, sex work. Only certain stages celebrate flamboyance and provide an income. Tennessee Williams had this down to a 't', but it, too, cost him. Or, at least it did so for Sebastian in *Suddenly Last Summer* (1958) who is torn to pieces by a gang of youths in Spain. Sebastian's cousin Catherine is lobotomised for trying to tell the truth about his life. I wrote an invited obituary on Williams in 1983 for the first large format issue of the Australian national gay magazine *Outrage* (1983–2000). Rereading it, to my surprise I discover that there too I spoke of Crisp and Williams, with reference to their bashings and arrests. Williams wrote elsewhere of 'the grace with which one survives appalling experiences.'

Versions of these stories are legion, but there are also the stories of those who went elsewhere to take advantage of bigger cities where they could hone their skills, be away from family or gender expectations and find more room to move in their personal lives. For many Australians that city was London.

Australian performer Reg Livermore spent a year or so there in 1959. Shortly before he arrived, the London Hippodrome had been converted into a cabaret restaurant, 'Talk of the Town'. He immersed himself in theatre, the latest musicals and touring: dancing, singing, and acting. Back in Australia he established himself. In the late sixties he appeared in both the Sydney and Melbourne versions of *Hair* and in 1972 he played Herod in *Jesus Christ Superstar*. When the show moved to Melbourne from Sydney, he wanted to change how his role was performed:

> I wanted to rise-up out of the petals of the Brian Thomson designed decahedron, just like Jesus did in the first half, but my entrance would be more like Shirley Bassey coming up out of the floor at the Talk of the Town in London.

I saw Livermore in the *Rocky Horror Show* in 1974 at the New Arts Cinema in Glebe Point Road, Sydney, with Wiebke Störtenbecker and other friends. It was my first systematic exposure to a man in a slinky corset, purpose built very high heels and fishnet stockings. He modelled himself on Bette Davis and strutted the stage as Frank 'n' Furter. Jim Sharman directed and Brian Thomson designed. I'd like to say I left the theatre a changed man, but as gob smacked and delighted as I was, it wasn't that simple. Though I did go back and see it twice more, I still had a long way to go.

Other homosexuals, both those with money and those without, had earlier gone to Paris (Gertrude Stein, Janet Flanner) or Berlin, and some eventually from Britain to the USA. After WWII think Marrakesh, Tangier, Capri, Ibiza, Tunis, Alexandria. Many were writers. James Baldwin first went to Istanbul in 1961 saying he could not breathe as a black man in the USA. He finished *Another Country* there soon after and stayed on and off for a decade. Not all trajectories were the same. Others were left activists involved in progressive politics. The Australian gay communist Denis Freney (1936–1995) records in his *A Map of Days* (1991) how he went to Algeria in 1963 after the war of independence to support what was occurring. In 1961, he had been to South Africa then in the steely grip of apartheid and the lead up to armed struggle. Later he was involved in the Vietnam War moratoriums, the protests against the Springbok rugby tour in 1971, the Gurindji peoples' struggle for land rights, Gay Liberation, and in the 1980s, the struggle for independence in East Timor. I still have some of the badges. I met Denis in Gay Liberation. He died from melanoma. I went to his funeral. Leaders of the struggle for Timor's independence were also there. I remember him with respect.

In Wilde's 1890 novel *The Picture of Dorian Gray*, Dorian wears Parma violets under his collar. Two years later, Wilde had one of the actors in *Lady Windermere's Fan* wear a dyed green carnation, as did several of his friends in the audience. Bartlett sees this form of homosexuality as a matter of 'laborious cultivation.' A defiant labour of love perhaps? At least for mischievous decadent aesthetes defending artificiality, it was the job of nature to imitate art. The audiences of Wilde's plays loved it. More staid English social observers saw this as a supercilious assertion of superiority. I would suggest that Wilde was challenging the English etiquette of politeness which hid multiple vicious private acts. It was a question of tactics. In Ed Madden's phrase the 'decadent cult of artificiality' was upon anglophones. It still hovers.

'Laborious cultivation': however artful, I am not a work of art. I just pick cultural pockets.

What some saw as flaunting unnatural behaviour was for others an insistence space be made for them. Often enough that involved coded behaviour.

26

What does one need to do to survive with some integrity and resist the forces of darkness? Defensiveness gets a bad press in these matters. Some battles are not military.

We are but a step away from pansies and the dyed green carnations that I have seen Leigh wear on occasion. He once also went to Sydney's Gay and Lesbian Mardi Gras wearing a blood-stained costume like that worn by the then Jacqueline Kennedy in the back seat of the car when President Kennedy was shot. I was initially taken aback by the refusal of tastefulness involved, then delighted. Bad taste has its own pleasures, as John Waters and Divine have taught us, over and over.

Knowingly or not, over time one cultivates a self. Friends are often part of this process. We try out ways of thinking and being with each other, make things conscious, adapt our behaviour, or not. Other times we might do it through a considered relation with objects.

My first exposure to the concept of 'taste' was through a Latin tag that I heard in a seminary in 1969 or 1970, *de gustibus non disputandum est*: 'concerning taste there is no dispute'. Taste, it declared, was irrevocably subjective and, by implication, not worth extended discussion. *Finis*. People liked what they liked. It puzzled me. I had vaguely intuited that taste was something to which one was supposed to aspire. I wasn't interested particularly in being refined, but another student spoke of the Australian artists Charles Blackman and Fred Williams of whom I had never heard, as well as of Proust and Thomas Mann, and I wanted to know more. Much of the time I felt ignorant and found aesthetic standards baffling. I hadn't learned then the differences between being educated and being cultivated.

I was entering ever so slowly a naïve version of what Meaghan Morris (1992a) once referred to as the 'the high art/low life dualism'. It was only much later that I understood one could be culturally informed and enjoy the 'low life.'

I met my first boyfriend. He played rugby and liked musicals, especially *West Side Story*. He could sing. I read books: radical theology, James Baldwin, the *Village Voice*... In the seminary library, there were strange European philosophy texts by people with names like Husserl and Merleau-Ponty. I attribute their presence now to then Father John Burnheim who had studied at Louvain and taught Philosophy in the seminary in the late 1950s, before leaving first the seminary then the priesthood and the Church. After a time, he joined the Philosophy Department at Sydney University. I met him there. He later wrote of the seminary, 'There was no library of any use to which I had access.' I read these books like a recluse, hidden in a library. They offered another way of thinking, especially Merleau-Ponty,

> Our body is not in space like things; it inhabits or haunts space. It applies itself to space like a hand to an instrument. And when we wish to move about, we do not move the body as we move an object.
> (Merleau-Ponty in Edie 1964)

Not surprisingly, sex was furtive as we moved our bodies around haunted by the need for secrecy, inventive in our need. What else could it be in those circumstances? What did it mean to be in the world? Someone offered me Sartre's novel, *Nausea* (1938). It matched my emotional state. That was followed by *Existentialism and Humanism* (1946). Existence precedes essence: to do is to be.

I left the seminary on the weekend of my twenty-first birthday in October 1970. A small group of seminary friends came to my birthday dinner,

Chinese takeaway, a special treat delivered from Liverpool to the Holsworthy army camp in outer south western Sydney. I lived with my parents again for maybe two months. In 1971, I spent a year in the Commonwealth public service and lived in the inner suburb of Glebe briefly before moving to Wyndham Street, Redfern. I was moved out of the Commonwealth Employment Service office in North Sydney to Youth Services in Central Office after refusing to continue checking that the young male job seekers had registered for conscription. My then boyfriend and I 'necked' in the darkness of the back row watching Ken Russell's *Women in Love* in (perhaps) a George St picture theatre, followed by what seemed to me a posh dinner in Martin Place at one of the Cahill's restaurant chain outlets. It's odd what watching Alan Bates and Oliver Reed wrestle in the flickering shadows of an open fire could do then to one's appetite. Glenda Jackson won the Oscar. Bates was gay, but I doubt we knew that. Not long after, someone pinched my 100cc motor bike. That was the year I had a suit made for $20 and matched it with a white polo-necked dinner shirt. I ate frogs' legs and snails at Chez Madeleine's in Liverpool St, just above Whitlam Square, though the square wasn't named that until 1983.

The following year I took leave from the public service, became a student again and made my way into the Gay Liberation Group at Sydney University. It was 1972. I was reading Theodore Roszak's *The Making of a Counter Culture* (1969). Now an Emeritus Professor, but then a lecturer in politics, Dennis Altman had set it with others for the subject Government II. I was beginning to understand the world around me. I went on the Aboriginal Ningla-A-Na (Hungry for Land) marches in Sydney and anti-Vietnam war demonstrations. I ordered Altman's *Homosexual. Oppression and Liberation*

(1971) from Gay Sunshine Press in San Francisco. I had to screw up my courage to get the bank cheque made out to them. About six weeks later it arrived on my doorstep in Ashfield. I sat up all night reading it, excited, confused, informed, enticed. Around then I began wearing tie dyed shirts.

By the later 1970s, I was increasingly interested in how value congregated around cultural preferences. Some of that interest had been prompted by meeting Drusilla Modjeska in 1975. She was writing her PhD on Australian women writers and would go on to write *Exiles at Home* (1981). In 1982 Drusilla asked me to teach Recent Australian Writing at the NSW Institute of Technology for a semester, and to speak about the urban novel at a Sydney History Group conference on the city and the creative arts. I had been doing work on Christina Stead, Eleanor Dark, Kylie Tennant and others for my Masters. I spoke about the city as place and metaphor. There I met Elizabeth Webby who was to become Professor of Australian Literature at the University of Sydney. Elizabeth later wrote an endorsement for the back cover of my book *A Guide to Gay and Lesbian Writing in Australia* (1996) as did Dennis, Robyn Archer, and Robert Dessaix. In different ways I am grateful to each of them.

In the early 1980s, Drusilla also asked me to do a small bit of research for a book she was editing with Marjorie Pizer on the poet Lesbia Harford. Shirley Walker my MLitt supervisor then put me on to Peter Pierce who shouted me coffee, picked my brain for his then forthcoming *Oxford Literary Guide to Australia* (1983) and acknowledged my input. I was on my way. Stepping stones. Like others, I was to have both successes and disappointments. In 1990 the editors of *My Looks Caress. A collection of modern romances* included my story 'A Nicotine Romance'. Robert Dessaix wanted to include it in his 1993 *Australian Gay and Lesbian Writing: An anthology* but was overruled.

In 1986 Kevin and I lived in Enmore in a house opposite Drusilla's. She was writing what became the highly successful *Poppy* (1990). Liz Jacka lived a few streets away in Newtown and was co-writing *The Screening of Australia* (1987) with Susan Dermody. The following year Liz and Susan co-edited *The Imaginary Industry. Australian film in the late '80s.* The three writers talked process together. I was watching, occasionally present. I had become part of networks asking why some cultural objects, films, books and authors for that matter were valued and taught and not others, why and how they were read or watched one way and not another and how might we read them? John Docker's *In a Critical Condition* (1984) had already opened my eyes to competing reading formations. My first academic book chapter appeared in Terry Threadgold and Anne Cranny-Francis' edited collection *Feminine, Masculine, Representation* (1990). I was working hard at getting my sergeant's stripes in post-structuralist analysis.

A while back, Drusilla and I crossed over briefly in London. After lunch, we went to a Japanese sock shop. I needed socks. With her encouragement, and some reluctance on my part, I bought two pairs at what I considered a shocking Soho price. Drusilla's eyes twinkled. She has particular tastes. I benefitted. The socks were cotton, thin, very well made and a sensual pleasure. I wore them for years till the onset of disintegration. No, not of me, the socks, though some might beg to differ. In writing this I am reminded to take delight in small things.

My takes are kaleidoscopic. I came of age in the period when the Australian Labor Party (ALP) lost

the 1969 election, won it in 1972 and 1974 and lost
it again in 1975 after the sacking of Whitlam. These
were the years of Black Power, Women's Liberation,
Gay Liberation, the end of the Vietnam war, the
struggle for land rights. Gender, race, nation, desire
and politics loomed ever larger in explanations
of cultural value, as did morality. In almost every
sense, it was also a matter of class, and of aesthetic
regimes and of institutional canons and cultural
capital: 'approved' taste, 'literary' taste, 'good' taste,
'simple' tastes. (It is rarely said of a vase that it is
'tasty', but it could be.) The Latin tag implies that
differences in taste are to be accepted, but much
depends on who is doing the acceptance, or not,
and how, and of what. 'There is no accounting for
taste' is often a sneer. Someone else's tastes are
thought to be deficient.

Even before then, in the 1960s, popular
culture had collapsed many of the old notions of
refinement. As Gail Hawkins put it in her entry on
'taste' in *New Keywords: A Revised Vocabulary of
Culture and Society*,

> Subcultural styles revealed the relationship
> between cultural choices and oppositional
> identity. Equally significant was the growth of
> fashion as a key site for the cultivation of the
> self and the practice of an everyday aesthetic.

Several months after I left the seminary, I returned
to visit remaining classmates, including Kevin. We
have been friends ever since, almost fifty years. I
wore purple flares and an orange shirt, probably
bought at The House of Merivale and Mr John in
Pitt St., Sydney. It was Easter Sunday, 1971. The
Rector of the College scuttled around the corner
in soutane and biretta in his haste to get away
from visually disruptive visitors. Once I wore them

too. A biretta is a three or four cornered square black cap with a tuft on top. We bought them at Pellegrini's in George Street. A soutane is a cassock. That doesn't help? Think a neck to ankle thick black dress buttoned all the way down the front. In 1968, Thomas Keneally, an earlier ex-seminarian, had won the Miles Franklin Award for his first novel, *Three Cheers for the Paraclete*. My favourite line has always been, 'It's your episcopal ring we are supposed to kiss, my Lord.' The lord, in this instance, being a bishop.

In Northern Ireland at that same time in the early seventies, during the Troubles, people could be arrested for wearing khaki combat jackets. Under the Special Powers Act, they constituted a paramilitary uniform.

Clothing is both a commodity and a signifier of stylistic differences between and amongst people of all classes. It has a social value. On Sundays in the 1950s and '60s, at least in regional Australia, one wore one's best to church. Often enough for some of us, some of the time, that was a modified version of our school uniform – grey long trousers or a pleated skirt. Anything more was of higher status and appeared only on very special occasions. Home dressmaking was often evident in the process. Respect and respectability went hand in hand with low incomes, but increasingly commodity culture penetrated everyday life. Now there are styles of living. McMansions in outer suburban developments are but one example. They connote taste for some, and success and upward mobility, all measured by newness and space. 'New' is mandatory, again for some, and 'innovative' is what matters to others. Still, others, don't give a damn. Except when they get the bathroom done and suddenly want modern plumbing or a specific kind of tile, a 'look'. These products (clothes, houses,

furniture) allocate status and preference ('value')
differently and differentiate discontinuities in class
politics. A new Holden took you a long way in 1950s
and 1960s regional Australia, as did a Ford Zephyr.

For many people, maybe most of the time,
liking something – a cup, say – is enough. The same
people, however, are just as likely to have a special
interest: ska, soul, film noir, manga, pub rock,
home maintenance, the gym, martial arts, cycling,
golf, Laminex furniture, cottage gardens, coins,
workwear, special objects. Then the story changes
because it is the signified that matters – their
preferred activity or interest is their 'real' interest
and the stories they tell in relation to whatever it is.
It is that which made the ABC's *The Collectors* and
the BBC's *Antiques Roadshow* long-term popular
hits. They are part of everyday life for many. One
of my interests is in how various objects are given
social value. Another is in how sometimes, politics
are, can or might be articulated in relation to them.

As a small child, it was books I turned to
for stories. I grew up with hardbacks. My first
present that I remember was a book, Dorothy
Wall's Australian children's classic, *Blinky Bill*. My
mother and I were both members of the Wodonga
library, forever overshooting the return-by date.
Reading was valued for entertainment (especially
before television) and later for education, or
at least information: Arthur Mee's *Children's
Encyclopaedia*. The pictures of puffins fascinated
me. They are now globally endangered.

I had no sense of a literary canon being
involved in book selection, and at least until
secondary school read relatively indiscriminately.
I still do quite often. Reading was also a chance
to escape into private worlds, and a revelation
that other things and ways of being were possible.
French literary theorist Roland Barthes said it is

the giving of value, what one does when 'reading', that determines meaning, not the intention of the author. In the process of reading or watching, meaning is given also to form. Form distinguishes novels from plays, film noir from melodrama (well, sometimes) in the name of genre. When some Art Deco designers gave cups triangular handles, they in effect challenged utility as the only or primary characteristic of a cup handle. Some dismissed this as silly, some were delighted, and others couldn't have cared less. It's a cup for chrissake. Pass me that mug. Yes, that one; it holds more. The thing is, though, some of us are willing to accept less functional cups in the interests of delight, at least for display purposes. However, there is no need to push the discussion to extremes. There are perfectly usable, well-designed cups.

The first time I discussed cup handles was in 1975. My friend Julie Bishop – no, not that one – spoke about porcelain china and the need for a handle you could get your finger through. It is a recollection that comes slowly after I see Julie several times between 2009–2017. In my case, memory seeps in as well as out. I then begin to wonder about my Royal Doulton cup and saucer that is not in the cabinet. Did Julie give me that, or was it, perhaps Di Holdway? I ask Julie next time I see her and show her a photo of the Doulton cup and saucer that happens to be on my phone. It rings no bells, but she wonders whether she may have given me a Deco cup. Does a colour come to mind I ask? Julie pauses, and says yellow. I recall that in the kitchen cupboard where I keep most of the china that is not in the cabinet, there is a paper-thin porcelain Deco cup, saucer and plate decorated with a grey and yellow squares pattern. When I get home, I'll photograph the cup and send the photo to her. Sometimes even long-term memory drops out, and I need every prompt I can get. I think of it as buffering.

A month later, back in Melbourne, I send the photo to Julie and she remembers the pattern. The pieces are stamped 'Victoria Fine China. Made in Bohemia'. I am very pleased. They mark the longevity of our friendship. I cannot ask Di about the Royal Doulton cup as she died in 2001. 'The Di Holdway Collection' in Sydney's Powerhouse museum is a collection of artful political posters produced in the Tin Sheds at the University of Sydney, during the 1970s and 1980s. Di, Virginia Heywood and I saw the film adaptation of E.M. Forster's novel *Maurice* together in London in the late 1980s or early 1990s. Forster is remembered for saying in various ways 'only connect'. We did.

Each of us by then lived far apart. Di had been in north Queensland and the Northern Territory. Virginia was ensconced in London. I was back in Sydney. Connection took various forms and was sometimes coincidental: crossover on trips to London, phone calls, messages or news passed on by others.

We had also connected on dance floors. The 1974 May Day Revolution Ball brought many of us together in the Balmain Town Hall, Sydney. Colin Little's bold multi-coloured poster had the Phantom and Groucho and Karl Marx leading us on the long march to the music of the Captain Matchbox Band and Blatant Outrage. Mao tailed off to the left. UFOs flew overhead. Acidic surrealism at its best. Three years later in 1977, Chips Mackinolty and the Earthworks Poster Collective produced the poster for the Second Triennial May Day Palace Revolution Ball. It too is in Di's Powerhouse collection. This time two women led the parade and the music came from the bands, Sheila, Wasted Daze and Stiletto. Both posters exhorted punters to come as their favourite faction. In the 1977 poster, the then Prime Minister Malcolm Fraser lay dead in the foreground. All proceeds went to the Right to Work campaign. The counter culture had faded. Life had got tougher.

Chips' parents and Chips himself were very kind to me when I was distraught after the memorial for Helen Golding in the Redfern Town Hall in 1978. I had come up from Melbourne to be there. Helen had died in a car accident at the end of Easter on her way to work at an Aboriginal legal service in regional New South Wales. She had shared a house with Peter Murphy and John Terry, where I had spent occasional nights with John. I recently discovered Lesley Podesta was at the memorial too, but I did not meet her until the following year after she moved to Melbourne and we began to share a house with others. Friendship circles sometimes involve serendipity.

A few months after Helen's memorial Peter was badly bashed by police at the first Mardi Gras in the cells of Darlinghurst police station. He finds it hard to speak about still, but he does. Chips was a straight political activist and ally. Di was too. They were amongst the people present at various points on the night of that first Mardi Gras, as were Julie and Craig Johnston, when the police attacked in King Cross and again outside and inside Darlinghurst police station. Chips and the Earthworks Poster Collective also designed the poster for the 1979 Gay Solidarity Week in Sydney. The banner depicted in the poster read 'Repeal all Anti Homosexual Laws. End Police Harassment of Homosexuals.' Solidarity, camaraderie and police thuggery. Forty years later in 2018, the Police Commissioner apologised to the '78ers for the police violence.

John was a lawyer. Leigh also knew him. We too only discovered that much later.

Craig, Julie and I had met at Sydney University in 1973. On Julie's first day at university she had gone to a history lecture and sat next to Monica whom I then knew well. They introduced themselves to each other and later that day Monica introduced me to Julie. Shortly after, I met Craig perhaps at a student democratisation meeting in the Department of Government or a meeting about whether the Government Department would support the strike in the Philosophy Department over whether a course in feminism could be taught and by whom. It eventually was and I took it as a subject. They were heady times. In October that year Julie, Craig and I were at a Builders Laborers Federation demonstration in defence of a green ban on urban renewal in the historic area of Sydney known as the Rocks. The redevelopment authority had hired non-union labour to break the ban. Craig was arrested along with fifty-seven others, including the BLF leaders, Jack Mundey, Joe Owens and Bob Pringle. I was aghast at the sight of Craig being roughly bundled into a paddy wagon. It was my blooding in street militancy. We had been at other demonstrations during the year but at this one the police had turned even nastier than usual. Julie was 18, Craig was 22 and I had just turned 24. Peter may have well been there too.

Ken 'Joe' McClelland had introduced me to Leigh in 1982 at the Eighth National Conference of Lesbians and Gay Men in Canberra. Ken had driven us up from Melbourne. Leigh was at a table distributing the journal *Gay Information* and other materials. He once said he thought we had met before that. He could be right of course. We met again in Sydney after the conference. Leigh and I grew closer after I came back to Sydney in 1985. In 1987 as I was heading home from the University of Technology on Broadway, I bumped into him. I'm going to Europe in late November, he said. On the spur of the moment I asked whether I could go with him. Yes, he said generously. We flew out several months later: London, Barcelona, Amsterdam.

In Barcelona Leigh bought tickets to Arrigo Boito's opera *Mefistofole*. I had never heard of Boito or of the female lead, Montserrat Caballé, much less the male singers. I suspect now that I had been to an opera only once before, with Jan McKemmish in 1982. We had come back early from fishing on Currarong beach to see the Kurt Weill/Bertolt Brecht opera the *Rise and Fall of the City of Mahagonny*, directed by Richard Wherrett in the Sydney Opera House. I was totally absorbed by it. We sat in the back row of the circle. In the Barcelona Opera House (the Gran Teatro del Liceu) the seats were in the front row of one of the highest tiers, much closer to the central ceiling dome than the stage. (As we discuss our recollections of this event Leigh tells me that the upper tiers are referred to colloquially as 'hen roosts'. We laugh.) The moment we went to our seats my lurking fear of heights flared acutely. I listened to the first aria in a state of barely managed panic, and as the audience applauded, I made my exit from mid-row with my back to the stage bending over other patrons out of fear that otherwise I would fall. There was muttering as I passed with much embarrassment. I retreated to a little gay bar in a lane off the Plaça Reial, then a quite dangerous area just off Las Ramblas. Leigh met me hours later. I was not in a good state shall we say. The bar became our regular haunt, as did for Leigh the Café de L'Opera. A very camp regular at the bar took to mocking us whenever we arrived: "Cup of tea, English women?" with right hand raised and little finger curled.

Leigh also tells me that in honour of Wilde we drank absinthe. While I might have heard of absinthe, I doubt I had ever drunk it. It was barely available anywhere in Europe other than in Spain, and generally known only to those with bohemian tastes. The regular mocker also sold us raffle tickets for a Christmas hamper every time we arrived. It hung from a net attached to the ceiling. He was raising money for People Living with AIDS. Early on, he warned us off, in Leigh's terms, 'the conspicuously handsome barman' largely on the basis that the barman was a non-Catalan from Seville.

Sensing my growing openness to opera, in 1989 Craig gave me a ticket to Donizetti's *Lucia di Lammermoor*, again at the Sydney Opera House. Before that, Kevin had been trying for years to get me interested in opera, as had Leonie Millar in Melbourne before him. Maybe I went to *Madame Butterfly* with Leonie. I had listened to it with her several times. What's not to like in Un Bel Di ('One Fine Day')? I was an inconstant opera pupil. I still am, but I began to appreciate operatic forms. Sometime after our separate returns to Sydney, Leigh became the opera critic for the *Sydney Star Observer* and other publications. On occasion I benefitted from a complimentary ticket and his knowledge, as I did from that of others, like Liz and Marion Jacka, and Gary Dowsett. Wagner sidled into view, but I never invited him to stay overnight. I did, however find the 1993 Sydney Opera House revival of *Tristan and Isolde* totally engrossing and admired yet again Brian Thomson's set design. Much of the stage was taken-up with a shallow, low-walled pool reflecting the lighting and an angled perspex overhead wing. Singers came and went from darkness. Simple, stark, haunting. The 1990 version had been conducted by Stuart Challender. He died of AIDS in 1991. A week after his death I went with Leigh at his invitation to Challender's memorial service in Sydney Town Hall. Accompaniment too has its own forms.

Over the years Julie and I have met, drunk coffee or been tourists together in Sydney, Melbourne, London, Berlin and Istanbul. I need no prompting to remember this. We wandered, paused and ruminated for hours in the archaeological museum in the grounds of the Topkapi Palace. I have eaten in her home with Sean Kidney, their children, their friends, and smoked on the deck that on a clear night allows me to see ten kilometres south to the Shard. Julie and Sean introduced me to Highgate Wood and we later wandered the Heath, much in the same way as I have done with Virginia who took me to the leafy serenity of Abney Park Cemetery in Stoke Newington in the late eighties. We go there still when we are both visiting London at the same time. On a recent foray there I went with Susan Ardill who was also visiting and met her and Wendy's son Oliver. Together we too meandered its paths. Susan is a Mardi Gras 1978er who was part of the early Gay Waves radio programme on 2SER FM in Sydney before going to London in the early 1980s and writing and editing for the feminist magazine *Spare Rib*. She produced two series of *Out on Tuesday*, the world's first gay and lesbian TV series, for Channel 4 in Britain. At other times I have wandered Abney Park alone. It closes at dusk.

Once again in Stoke Newington, in 2010 I watched the World Cup finals on TV with Terri Bednall in her flat. Vuvuzelas blared from the crowd almost drowning out the commentary, but not quite the traffic noise from the High Street some floors below. We drank tea, laughed a lot, cheering as needed. Spain defeated the Netherlands, but I forget for whom we barracked. The spectacle was enough. The Kurdish barber in the High Street waxed my nose and ears as part of a haircut. That was a first. Quite startling, as he had not said he was going to do it and wax is hot. Somewhat smarter, in new black boots that almost crippled me, I went from Terri's flat to Will Nutland and Aaron Balick's civil partnership ceremony in Islington Town Hall. The boots sit still and dusty in my wardrobe even now.

In 2017 Virginia shows me the Islington section of the New River Path that runs below Upper St Islington toward Canonbury Overground station. The New River was an aqueduct built in the early seventeenth century to supply water to north London. Technically it is neither new nor a river, but that is another story. A few weeks after Virginia shows it to me and discusses its history, I walk it again, this time with Lynne Segal. Affection is strengthened with sociable rambling.

Friendships are social relations made more or less apparent in manifold shared activities, in gifts, staying in touch, remembering and forgetting, invitations, but also in the setting of boundaries, in refusals and in emotional reactions that enhance, complicate or challenge. They are responsive and interactive. I make friends, I share them. Sometimes they fade. I occasionally lose them. Most gay men and their friends of my generation have gaps in their lives where other friends were. The dead are many.

My relations with objects are similarly multi-layered. Gifts can be delightful, pleasing, puzzling or misplaced. The object involved in the giving can have its own claim to specialness based on its material characteristics which may elicit a response, remind, celebrate. Material specialness – artistry: the feel, the look that comes with the play of light, design – is in this context imbued with the thoughtfulness of the giver in choosing an object likely to please.

42

Cultivation is a practice of social as well as aesthetic stylisation and plays out on many fields, in schools, in lounge rooms, in social networks, in writing, in art, in film, in sex, in the light, in the dark. I learned as a boy what was too girly to say, though I kept an unhealthy interest in horse novels for longer than I was supposed to. The early novels in Elyne Mitchell's Silver Brumby series (1958–1999) set in Australia's Snowy Mountains were clearly the beginnings of my downfall. Only girls liked horses. Boys worked with them. The school playground was beset with traps. One of them snapped shut: Hurley rhymes with girly. I persisted with reading in my bedroom.

As a pubescent teenager, I read my mother's English magazines *Woman's Day* and *Woman's Own*. I suspect for her they represented 'home'. To me, they were somehow exotic. They often featured Cecil Beaton's fashion photography. I have a vague memory of being bemused by women's hats and white gloves. I read the advice columns. *Women's Own* featured Beverly Nichols (1898–1983) as a regular columnist from 1946–1967. Playwright Alan Bennett considers Nichols' columns a possible source of his mother's claim to 'a sort of refinement.' Joshua Adair refers to Nichols as 'a prominent English tastemaker.' Interior decoration and home-making link him largely backwards to Oscar Wilde and in Nichol's case a valorising of eighteenth-century country life. He queered domestic space, making it public as in a sense only men of a certain kind and class could do. Women were stuck with it, even when they also did paid work.

In February 1965, I watched Winston Churchill's funeral on black and white television with my father. We sat largely in silence. I recall the measured stately pace of the gun carriage carrying the coffin through London from Westminster Hall to St Paul's cathedral. The commentary refers to 'the great commoner.' It is said smoothly, authoritatively from deep within the sureties of a constitutional monarchy. 'Commoner', someone who is not an aristocrat. It is true Churchill had no title, but his father and paternal grandfather did. He came from the aristocracy. The Marxist cultural theorist Raymond Williams spoke of cultures having three simultaneous dimensions, residual, dominant and emergent. Constitutional monarchies have ensured that residual traps and trappings preserve legal, political and social powers. Tradition weighs heavily. The Irish disestablished the Church of Ireland in 1871. The Welsh disestablished in 1920 and the Scots in 1929. The monarch, however, is still titular head of state of the United Kingdom and head of the Anglican Church. The House of Lords is appointed, not elected. It has made me appreciate much more French republicanism and its insistent separation of church and state. Their nobles have no official legal status.

Watching Churchill's funeral was a rare moment. My father spoke with me perhaps for the first time as though I was vaguely adult. It made me very uncomfortable. I didn't want to be his confidante. I cannot know what Churchill's death meant to him, but I suspect now it marked the beginning of an ending of his tie to an English past. Kind of. The event was also momentarily pulling him back to his origins. It was after all a funeral, and on reflection he was quite affected. His mother told me on a visit to Australia in 1969–70 that her husband, my grandfather, had been reported dead at Gallipoli. He reappeared a year later. Like Churchill, someone had got it wrong.

My mother went back to England for the first time in the mid-1970s to see her family. By then both her parents were dead. After she came back,

I never heard her call England 'home' again. That is not to say she did not. Me, I was born there. I am a dual citizen, for the moment anyway. I visit London willingly. I have good friends there, but it is not home for me either. Except it haunts me, especially on matters of culture, race and social difference. The good times happen despite those who still declare its greatness as they angrily mourn its decline.

I back track a moment to my phrase 'men of a certain kind.' Charles Hawtrey and Kenneth Williams in the *Carry On* films were probably my first cinematic exposures to male homosexual personas, albeit coded in terms of eccentric male characters enacting a strangely stylised lack of blokey masculinity. Syd James provided the bluff bloke contrast, just. One commentator refers to Hawtrey's 'natural campness... that he explored to its limits'. They were funny, but it would never have occurred to me that I might behave like that, much less want to. Not in Bandiana army camp where we climbed hills, trapped rabbits and I fished alone along Wodonga Creek with Watson's Hill at my back. Nor indeed did I understand then what I was seeing in Hawtrey's acting. What I did sense was that I couldn't be publicly odd, strange or unusual. Privately, I was already peculiar. Army camps are about rank, orders and obedience. For that and other reasons I learned increasingly to be silent. A child does not speak until spoken to. Speech was dangerous.

I was learning caution every which way I turned. Life wasn't a film, though later I did have a crush on Troy Donahue. I had no named sense of what it meant. Yes, I went on to have girlfriends. I knew how to kiss and learned how to fumble, but not how to make social conversation. I also had silent inchoate crushes on boys. Caution was intuitive,

rather than a simple matter of conscious denial,
elemental. I wandered paddocks alone, watching the
swallows fly in and out of their mud made nests in
the viaduct under a disused railway line.

Long before Mitch gave me the Susie Cooper
cup and saucer, perhaps in the mid 1990s, she had
given me two Ruth Boden bone china mugs that
celebrated fish and fishing – one had a Rainbow
Trout on it, the other a Grayling. I use them still,
every day. Each of the mugs has a fishing fly on the
inside. The fly in the trout mug is called Wickham's
Fancy. The Grayling mug has a Red Tag fly in
it. Mitch called me in Sydney from Melbourne
sometime in the early nineties and suggested we
meet on the NSW south coast and head out past
Dalgety for a couple of days of fishing. We did. Years
later I wrote for her birthday:

> On the Newmerella River at Nimmitabel
> in the rain shadow of the mountains
> kingfishers dived
> and you and the angling man flipped artificial flies over
> water so clear and fast
> that the still-edged pool on the other side seemed a mirage
> of heat and mirrors.
> Even dragonflies thought twice about landing

I fished with a spinner or perhaps bait, way
outclassed. Fly fishing is for wrist flicking adepts.

Sometime in the late eighties we had danced
with other friends in a lesbian bar somewhere on or
near Tottenham Court Road, London, and again in
Ruby Reds in Crown St, Sydney.

> Whisky, hard floors, soft basement glows and in the
> morning eye-piercing sun.
> It was definitely the eighties.

46

Charles Hawtrey sometimes wore drag, but in the tradition of music hall and variety shows drag did not always indicate the performer was gay. They often were however, and Hawtrey was, but heterosexual men also cross-dressed and impersonated women, and presumably enjoyed doing so. Barry Humphries as Edna Everage is but one example. The Sea Horse Club in Sydney in the 1960s and 1970s had a very mixed assortment of 'transvestite' members, mostly straight I was told at the time. Cross-dressing is sometimes discussed as gender bending, but Hawtrey performed a non-standard version of masculinity rather than attempting to 'pass' as female. One always knew he was a man. It was masculinity he bent, not the gender system unless you see them as the same thing. His drag wasn't meant to be convincing. Mostly the variety involved innuendo and double entendre – *Carry on up the Khyber*.

Khyber Pass – arse.

I did not just read books, I also read the *Weekly Times*. It was geared to rural readerships. I looked at the prices of land and cows, sheep and tractors in the classifieds and fantasised life as a dairy farmer. Friesians produced the most milk, but Jerseys were the richest in cream. It was an innocent enough preoccupation. I was often up at 6am to herd everyone's house cows up to the bails to be milked, by hand, with my peers. We took it in turns to bring them in or take them back. Barefooted in the frost, I thought I might be a vet. Vocational testing, a few years later, was to say otherwise. I started reading Dickens. Magwitch stumbles out of the mist and Pip is scared stiff. So was I. We didn't have crib notes. That was the teacher's job. Poverty produces crime, imprisonment, transportation to Australia. Pip, back in London, benefits unknowingly from Magwitch's labours.

One person's transportation is another's (ongoing) experience of invasion. Dickens published *Great Expectations* in 1861. Transportation ended in 1868. Massacres of the Indigenous peoples continued, as did slavery.

1868 was also the year of the last hangings for sodomy in Tasmania. They had ceased in NSW in 1836. The last one in England was in 1834, though it remained on the statute books for longer.

Twenty years or so after *Great Expectations* was published, Wilde was linking aesthetics with contemporary life. He spoke into the present, looked forward, though often enough history was his guide. On his lecture tour of the USA in 1882, Wilde's public presentations constantly changed and developed but generically included 'The English Renaissance', 'The Decorative Arts', 'The House Beautiful', 'Dress'. He took domestic interiors seriously.

Wilde had studied at Oxford under Walter Pater who in his *Studies in the History of the Renaissance* (1873) had promoted an intense engagement with beauty.

The Meissen cup and saucer that sit on the top shelf of the china cabinet next to the Susie Cooper set 'Recumbent Deer' are from Meissen's Cosmopolitan mesh gold series. While the coffee cup is white, the saucer is decorated with a fine fawn mesh pattern. The centre of the saucer where the cup sits is also white. The cup is of contemporary modern design, quite formal, classic in its simplicity, functional. There is plenty of room for a strong finger grip to steady and hold it in one's hand, yet the handle is neither a simple curve nor sharply angled. The bottom of the handle projects out at perhaps forty degrees before a slight curve raises it vertically until another gently rising curve turns it again towards the cup. Underneath, both

48

cup and saucer are marked with Meissen's crossed swords, a branding Meissen instituted in 1722.

Meissen claims to be the first European company to have cracked the porcelain code. Aristocracies had been importing porcelain from China at great expense for about four hundred years, before Meissen set up its Porcelain Manufactory in 1710. Gary Dew walks me through the process: 'at a certain point when you heat clay at a high temperature its chemical composition changes, and it is not clay any more. It becomes pottery, porcelain.' Bone china is a variant of soft-paste porcelain and is known for its whiteness and translucency. It includes bone ash. 'Fine Porcelain' was first produced in England in Bow, East London, in the mid 1700s, then in 'New Canton' on the river Lea, before being further refined by Josiah Spode senior in the 1790s. Its production largely occurred in Stoke-on-Trent. His son renamed 'Stoke China' as 'Bone China'.

These are threads and dregs that traverse colonial worlds in the nineteenth century and beyond. In 2014 Australia was fourteenth internationally in per head tea consumption. Turkey was first and the UK third. Turkey began producing its own tea when it became a secular republic under Mustapha Kemal Ataturk in 1923. There had been a time when Australians were the highest per head consumers of tea, but that had changed by the 1950s.

I recall my mother offering me coffee one night in the late 1950s as we listened to the radio, perhaps the Jack Davey Show. Davey died in 1959. His biographer Lesley Johnson reports that somewhere between 100,000–150,000 people stood in pouring rain in Sydney for his funeral. The coffee was made from a bottle of Robur or Bushells liquid coffee and chicory essence. That was new. So was the portable transistor I won a couple of years later in an Albury radio competition.

II

The objects in my IKEA cabinet are personal memorabilia, keepsakes. Their preciousness is affective, separate from any assessment of their tastefulness or market value. Curiosities, if you like, yet they also separately have public histories, like IKEA itself.

And me, for that matter. I have written and spoken publicly, on and off, for about fifty years. I reference some of it here as I go. Writing about my china took me quite by surprise. I never have before and had no idea I wanted to until it happened. An unexpected me emerged. I was writing myself through my relation to objects. Lynne Segal suggests in her *Out of Time* (2013) that the time we feel most at one with the world is often when we are in a sense *least* our ordinary selves.

Cups can have multiple histories that also take me by surprise. My academic and activist friend Dino Hodge has a set of four seventies Mikasa Duplex yellow coffee cups. They are unmarked but are designed by Ben Seibel. The top halves of the cylindrical cups flare gently out. They have a dint in their bottoms. The saucers have raised centres that fit into the dints and stabilise them for carrying. Mikasa was an American import-export house influenced by Japanese design. The brand was attached to outsourced china manufactured in several countries including Japan. Mikasa became popular in Australia sometime in the later sixties and the brand was bought out by the French group Arc International in 2000. Dino's pieces are engagingly simple. During an afternoon catch up, he and I drink tea out of the cups. What matters is not that it is tea rather than coffee, nor how the tea tastes (quite acceptable) but the event itself: a convivial sipping as we sit discussing cup design and his upcoming trips. It is not exactly campfire territory, and there are no cattle lowing in hearing distance, but it is late afternoon on a hot day, and a bloke knows a hot sip will cool him down.

Aesthetics and aestheticism too have histories, often, in the case of aestheticism, interrupted or rearranged by scandal. The English literary critic Cyril Connolly in his *Enemies of Promise* (1938) pointed to how the trial of Oscar Wilde 'was responsible for a flight from aestheticism which lasted twenty years.' Wilde – in the Marquess of Queensbury's viciously contemptuous term, that 'posing somdomite' (sic) – once said a version of 'either that wallpaper goes, or I do', and died a few weeks later. Wilde is a beacon for the aesthetically inclined. We like a good laugh, mordant and macabre, even as we speak against the laws of that time and acknowledge the social difficulties and personal pain of those who were most directly affected. Queensbury was cruel.

Connolly blamed marriage, alcohol and homosexuality for the limits of his own output as a young fiction writer. It is not a lot of eggs for a basket, though no doubt it was a heady combination.

Wilde's grave in Pere Lachaise cemetery, Paris, was entombed in glass in 2011–2012 to prevent lip-sticked fans kissing the marble, causing it to deteriorate. Grease had sunk into the marble. In the early sixties, vandals had chopped the genitals off Jacob Epstein's 1914 sculpture of a flying naked angel. Adam loves Steve, the graffiti said when I first saw it in 1988.

I hear Ella: Lipstick traces...

Almost sixty years after Connolly's remarks, Australian graphic artist and fashion designer David McDiarmid spoke (1993) and wrote (1997) of how one night in Sydney when back briefly from New York in the late seventies he had noticed 'a cluster of men dancing together who wore check shirts, 501s and military haircuts.' Many gay men had begun claiming a stylised working man's masculinity. McDiarmid remarked on how this

> confused those sisters whose model for being gay was precious, alcoholic and European ... "Haughtiness" had been replaced by "attitude".

The politics of butch had begun. McDiarmid's is a particular take on what was occurring. Others may well recall its history quite differently. The opposing of haughtiness with attitude is a knowing remark not an assertion of brute masculinity a la Stanley Kowalski in *A Streetcar Named Desire*. Attitude was a studied stance achieved by considerable effort in the gym and a considered adoption of working men's gear: not just check shirts, 501s and buzz cuts but also tight t-shirts, a moustache, sideburns. For others it was uniforms and leather, though many a wardrobe had all the options. The stance was everything, the strut, the look. It was an intervention, an assertion of sexual desire rather than romance, and in Sydney it became a communal politics.

The days of deep social isolation and fifties 'tea and sympathy' were almost over, at least for those in urban centres who knew about, and chose to explore, the burgeoning social options that constituted 'the scene'. In October 1979 Ivan Polson's *Klick!* Magazine reported that as Pokeys, a bar in The Prince of Wales Hotel in St Kilda, Melbourne, entered its third year, there were more than a thousand in attendance on Sunday nights. Richard Peterson reports more than half a million customers 'paid to see Pokeys between 30 October 1977 and 13 March 1992.'

That first part-sentence of McDiarmid's quoted above is a great cheap line with more than a grain of truth, combining as it does a campy wit with clone assertion. Simply put, there was and is more than one way of being and doing gay, however by the end of the seventies in Sydney and nationally there was a political struggle occurring around the formation of 'community'. The clone formation was arguably dominant culturally and politically in the western gay male project for the next decade if not two. In Australia it was central in the pre-AIDS articulation of 'community' especially in the face of the three police raids on the sex venue Club 80 in Sydney in 1983 when a thousand marchers protested. By then civil rights had permeated gay men's lives.

Gay liberation had segued into a movement and then a community, but for all the political tensions involved public voicing remained at its core. Collective solidarity was central in the initial response to HIV/AIDS. The moment AIDS emerged in Australia in late 1982 community activists began organising care and support and educational responses. Not all that long after they went to the federal government. Out of this came the bi partisan response to HIV and AIDS under the Hawke government, led by Labor's health minister Neal Blewett and the Liberals' shadow minister Dr Peter Baume. It made a major difference to what then occurred here compared to what happened in the UK and the USA.

'Preciousness' as seen in McDiarmid's remark means over refined: artificial, contrived, sometimes veering toward the twee, with maybe a hint of the theatrical, a touch of the 'girly'. Think Kenneth Williams on more acid drops and maybe, with a touch of cardigan – a sideways move from pastel pullovers – Proust and camomile tea. Well, let's be real, save the Proustian moments, memories generated over madeleines and tea, for a more literary dinner. Consider instead Dirk Bogarde's version of Aschenbach besotted and dying interminably on a Venice beach in Visconti's 1971 film version of Thomas Mann's *Death in Venice* – it is not a big step to take – and you realise it is a European literary homosexual imaginary and cultural heritage that McDiarmid most probably had in his sights. The Bogarde role was light years from Gary Oldman playing Joe Orton in Stephen Frears' 1987 film version of *Prick up Your Ears*.

McDiarmid bounced out of New York club land, honed on street sassiness and gay assertiveness. By the early 1990s when he first spoke 'A Short History of Facial Hair' he was speaking directly out of a militant HIV politics: 'That's Miss Poofter to you, asshole'. It was a period of rapidly rising deaths from AIDS – 'So many pills, so little time' – just two years before life-saving new therapies arrived.

His 1992 spiral bound book of computer-generated colour photocopies, *Toxic Queen*, had a self-published edition of 50 copies. It sold rapidly and became a collector's item. Impression 42/50 is held by the National Gallery of Australia (NGA). David died in 1995. I knew him slightly in those last years and went to his funeral with Leigh. It wasn't my or Leigh's first. Some of David's friends were wearing skull necklaces that he had made for the event not so long before he died. Along with Gillian Minervini and Ted Gott, composer and treatments activist Lyle Chan gave one of the eulogies: 'David's art was graphic', both artistically and sexually. McDiarmid dealt creatively and defiantly with sex, HIV/AIDS, treatments and death. His limited-edition compilation audio tape *Funeral Hits of the 90s* is also in the NGA. Lyle later composed *String Quartet: An AIDS Activist's Memoir in Music*.

This was all a long way from Albury and Wodonga in the 1960s.

I remember chortling with my mother in an Albury picture theatre in 1963 when I was about fourteen. We were the only two from the family there, a rare moment given I am the oldest of five children. The film was Robert Day's *Two Way Stretch* (1960), a prison comedy to the side of the better-known *Carry On* films and the later antics on TV of the *Benny Hill Show*. *Two Way Stretch* (there must be a double entendre there somewhere) starred amongst others Peter Sellers, Beryl Reid and Wilfred Hyde-White. Reid went on to star in the early lesbian play (1964) and film (1968) of *The Killing of Sister George*. She later played Connie Sachs in the classic BBC television series of John le Carré's novels *Tinker, Tailor, Soldier Spy* (1979) and *Smiley's People* (1982), series that riveted le Carré fans like Mitch and me. (The Berlin Wall and the Cold War had seven more years to run.) A superb interpreter of character, Reid began as a music hall performer in variety, a realm of English life and burlesque humour largely but not totally absent in George Orwell's takes of what mattered.

I believe it was the sexual innuendo that my mother and I enjoyed in *Two Way Stretch* even though we sat on the edge of discomfort in laughing about it together, in the dark, or at least I did. I can't speak for her. The plot probably mattered little.

[Fred's wife has brought in a young baby when she visits Fred in prison]
Fred: How old is he now, my love?
Fred's wife: Eight months, dearest.
[Fred looks suspicious and counts on his fingers]
Fred: But I've been in here nearly two years.
[Fred's wife smiles sweetly]
Fred's wife: Oh yes, Fred. But you sent me some *lovely* letters.

58

Clearly the letters were not French. A 'French letter' was a condom. The term was popularly used by English and Australian military personnel during WWII. It had largely died out in Australia by the mid 1970s.

The dialogue opens out a strange space. Innuendo, mock innocence and silliness vibrate together. That which is known – sex occurs and results in pregnancy – cannot be easily acknowledged or shared, except in the pleasure of laughter. What can be spoken, and how do you speak it? The pleasure of a good fuck was not so much vulgar, as taboo.

Le Carré's novel and Arthur Hopcraft's script for *Tinker Tailor* use the Cold War, and the fictionalised betrayals of Philby, Burgess and Maclean, to dramatise the sense of loss that accompanied the end of empire in the decades immediately after the war. Connie asks George Smiley to kiss her, and he does, ever so briefly. After the kiss, she says melancholically, not realising George is making his escape, and nostalgic for what was lost when she was pushed out of her job,

> Hey-ho halcyon days ... Trained to empire, trained to rule the waves. Englishmen could be proud then. They could, George. All gone. Bye, bye world.

Connie's grief is historicised. It is the 'Great' in Great Britain' she mourns. Her affection for George, the loss of her past employment and associated resentments reduce her to momentary melancholy. Hurt and resentment savoured with or without ice in a nice bit of crystal can have that corroding effect. Otherwise, she's as sharp as a tack.

Male homosexuality in the BBC *Tinker Tailor* directed by John Irvin is an intricate part of the le Carré version of spy services, in recruitment, in camaraderie, in love and betrayal. It is largely marked out by practices rather than identity – adjectival, as Gore Vidal insisted, rather than nominal – both homosocial and homoerotic. Smiley is trying to identify the Russian mole high up in the British secret service. (Think Kim Philby, but not too literally.) He speaks with a retired agent, Jim Prideaux.

> Smiley: *There's a letter Bill wrote about you to his tutor Fanshawe, a Circus talent spotter, in which Bill named you as suitable material for British intelligence. I can quote the odd line from memory:*
> "He has that heavy quiet that commands. He's my other half. Between us we make one marvellous man. He asks nothing better than to be in my company or that of my wicked, divine friends, and I'm vastly tickled by the compliment. He's virgin, about eight feet tall and built by the same firm that did Stonehenge."
>
> Prideaux: *Christ! Christ man we were children. What do you want to know?*

There is a history of respect and affection between these men, but it doesn't stop Smiley's implicit threat of blackmail. There's also warmth in how Bill Haydon spoke long ago of Prideaux with campy pride, admiration and love. Even so, Connie's 'boys' were not prone to playing nicely. Friendships were betrayed. At the end, Prideaux kills Haydon. Personal relations are both over-determined by and intertwined with the strategic vagaries of cold war operations, and forensic narration.

Affection, whatever its relations with objects or subjects, is not automatically nostalgia. The cold war homophobia narrative was sometimes more layered than many of the formal histories can tell us. The problem is one of cross referencing on-the-record documentation with material that fills in its gaps. It is not as though 'records' are innocent in what they include or exclude, gloss over, or sweeten. Le Carré knows enough to dramatize what was not officially recorded. He had been part of it. He also knows what makes for compelling storytelling in print and on screen.

In the televisual film version of *A Murder of Quality* (1991), scripted by le Carré from his 1962 novel and directed by Gavin Millar, a private school teacher on the verge of retirement tells the story of why he won't be getting a pension. He sought 'temporary consolation' in a 'cottage' and was entrapped by a policeman. The school said he could stay on as a temporary with no pension.

An attempt at 'temporary consolation' has resulted in a life squeezed by punishment, meanness, arbitrariness and the self-interested patronage of the powerful. It results understandably in moments of anger and self-pity. That is one form of the social relation we call tolerance and its effects. The thing is, however, it's also a plot moment in which the teacher is positioned as victim, and the audience is asked to identify, to sympathise with the historic unfairness, and look elsewhere for the murderer. But it is a whodunit, full of building dramatic tension, and, yes, the teacher did it. They are unreliable, these homosexuals. Dear reader, I just used the same narrative device as le Carré. Hang me. Buggery remained a capital offence in England and Wales until 1861.

A different aspect, but not always a separate one, is that of racial historicising. It is also

needed. British playwright Hanif Kureishi put it
this way in 1987,

> It is the British, the white British, who have to
> learn that being British isn't what it was.

I read this quote in the later 1980s about the time
I first saw Stephen Frears' film of *My Beautiful
Laundrette* (1985) in the Dendy Cinema in Martin
Place, Sydney. Kureishi wrote the film script. The
quote was like a punch to the solar plexus. The
film took my breath away. It set up a relationship
between two men, a British Pakistani and a
white British skinhead, living in an area where
the National Front had a street presence, and it
showed a range of ways British Pakistanis lived in
Thatcher's Britain and how women did and didn't
fit in. I was bowled over by those acts of social
inclusion, the acting and the film's stylistic bravura.
I wrote briefly about a kiss between the two men in
a short essay I included in *Two Timing. Sex, writing
and the writing of sex* (1991). They were kissing at
one end of an alley and the racist National Front
was at the other. This was a London I knew, albeit
slightly. There were anti-racist gay skinheads at my
favourite pub. A night or two before I left London
some of them took me home for my own protection.
　　In Derek Jarman's mesmerising take on
Thatcher's Britain, *The Last of England* (1987), a
skinhead stomps then writhes orgiastically on a
Caravaggio painting.
　　Britain, Pakistan, India, Sri Lanka, Jamaica
have all been part of each other for years. Kureishi
also said,

> It is strange to go away to the land of your
> ancestors, to find out how much you have in
> common with people there, yet at the same

time to realise how British you are . . . It isn't
what you wanted to find out.

There are some, very limited, similarities
between what Kureishi said and what Stuart
Hall wrote about in his posthumously published
autobiography *Familiar Stranger,* subtitled 'A life
between two islands'. Hall was Jamaican by birth
but emigrated to Britain in 1951. He had won a
Rhodes scholarship to Oxford university at 18. He
later became the founding editor of *New Left Review*
(1960), the first research fellow appointed to the
Birmingham Centre for Contemporary Cultural
Studies (1964) and the Centre's second director. Its
first director was Richard Hoggart, author of *The
Uses of Literacy* (1957). Hall concludes *Familiar
Stranger* with 'I wanted to change British society
not adopt it.' *Familiar Stranger* is a memoir of both
disjuncture and close engagement.
    Jamaica has its own history of Indigenous
dispossession and death by colonial diseases as well
of African slaves brought by the British to 'the pearl
of the Antilles.' Colin Grant (2017) in his review
of *Familiar Stranger* described local responses to
these situations this way,

> For [Marcus] Garveyites and eventually
> Rastafarians, Zion was Mother Africa. For the
> Anglophiles or Afro-Saxons of Hall's era, the
> mother country was Britain.

Hall's experiences are not of a Britain I knew.
He entered Britain a year before I was taken out.
I was taken aback as this writing proceeded to
find I was writing mostly about things European,
most often English, if not German. I am a post-
war child who lives in Australia and has dual
citizenship. I grew up in regional Australia on

both sides of the Murray River. I am proud of much but not all of its labour/union history and shamed and angered by its persistent racism. I would be the same way in England, but I would rather live here.

As a white British emigrant growing up in Australia, I had virtually no personal memories of the 'mother country', but without me realising until later, its cultural values governed my life. The education system ensured it, as did Australia's legal and political relationship with the British monarchy and the Commonwealth. That enculturation was very apparent to those who came from non-English speaking backgrounds, whether born here or not. Some sought to remedy it with Saturday language classes for their children. Dino referred to these classes in one of our conversations as Greek Sunday School. He has increasingly reverted to calling himself Konstantino Hadjikakou. I was 23 before I saw England again. I returned to London for some months over the summer break, 1973–1974, then again thirteen years later with Leigh, in 1987–1988. Two visits in almost forty years. Both times it had a surface familiarity ('The' Abbey and red double decker buses and things) but I had little local knowledge, and obviously came from elsewhere, where towns had funny names like Bandiana, Wodonga and Wagga Wagga. Mind you, Steeple Bumpstead or Bury St Edmunds provoke their own amusement. On that first trip, I carried my A–Z street directory everywhere I went. Now I use Google maps on the phone.

Wodonga is a Warajuri word meaning bulrushes. The area now known as Albury-Wodonga is the Warajuri people's homeland. They knew it as Bungam-brawatha.

By the time of my second visit to the UK, I was in my late thirties. Thatcher's wrecking ball was in full swing. There was a moment when I opened the thickly printed London phone directory, and for the first time saw on a map where my mother's family lived until after the war (Stepney) and where her father worked (Wapping), and then there, 'far' to the west, was Bristol my father's birth place, and south of London, Banstead in Surrey, where I was born. This, I suddenly realised, was where I came from. Well, sort of. It was my birthplace, but not my home. Later in that trip, after maybe a week or more in Florence, I found myself suffocating in the air of packaged heritage. I fled to Milan in the hope of a skyscraper. It was not to be, though there was much I came to admire. On the train there, looking out the window, I realised that every inch of the soil had been cultivated for millennia. It felt like a dead weight. I come, I thought, naively, and romantically, from the New World, and that is now my home. Except, of course, there was nothing new about Australia, other than for those of its people who had arrived in the previous two hundred years, me included, and the political and social systems they put in place.

I am as far as I know Anglo-Celtic. My ancestors on both sides came to England from Ireland during the Irish potato famine in the 1850s, itself a result of blight and British imperialism. I spoke English. My home life was English, and the kids I played were almost totally Australian-born. One friend was the son of an Australian father and a Japanese mother, a marriage legacy of WWII or perhaps Korea. In primary school, a few students began to arrive from the Bonegilla migrant camp, eight miles down the road. I spent some playtimes with Marietta from Finland. Others came from the Baltic states. I also recall Albert. We were school friends for a while. His parents were Dutch immigrants. I knew no Aboriginal people. At high school one of my closest friends was Greek. My father grew dahlias and rolled the manicured lawn. My mother spoke of 'home' and kept in touch with it through letters and parcels. I knew I had cousins, the children of her sisters and brother. I knew their names, but they were distant links, somewhere else. I met them on that first trip in the early seventies.

I was glad long years later that my father had made me do debating in High School, though that is not how I felt at the time, with my body shaking and face blushing at my temerity in speaking at all, much less publicly. It gave me practice in speaking despite my nervousness and diffidence. I could speak despite what I felt. I learned not to hold notes on paper in my hand. The sound of the paper fluttering as I shook amused the audience, but it embarrassed me further. Neither of my parents finished secondary school in their youth in England. My father went from school to an apprenticeship (fitting and turning) but did do an adult HSC in the mid-sixties, in the same year that I did the School Certificate. My mother had sung very occasionally in local choirs, sometimes in musicals. I learned to recognise 'Doing the Lambeth Walk' and heard of the Pearly Kings and Queens of East End tradition. 'South Pacific' was no longer all the rage. I had grown up with Elvis but the Brits were coming, again.

About the time that I read Dickens I also read Walter Scott's historical novel *Waverley* (1814) and instantly converted to what I considered the Scottish cause led by Bonny Prince Charlie (Charles Edward Stuart). To my mind, England was Perfidious Sassenach Albion. It was ten years or more before I realised that the attempt to regain the throne for the Stuarts also meant a restoration of Catholicism and was shocked at my ignorance.

At sixteen I was reading John Henry Newman's *Apologia Pro Vita Sua* (1845), his argument for why he left the Church of England for Roman Catholicism. At seventeen, while at High School in Albury, I too turned Catholic. After finishing the HSC, I also watched a double programme of Tennessee Williams' *Cat on a Hot Tin Roof* (Dir. Richard Brooks) and Mike Nichol's adaptation of Edward Albee's *Who's Afraid of Virginia Woolf* in the second of the two Albury picture theatres, off Dean St. It was the emotions I identified with. In the 1983 Tennessee Williams obituary I wrote of intensity taking hold 'like a leech in the dam and out-flooding the Murray.' The plots were beyond me. Adulthood, what was that? Between going to mass, working temporarily as a cheese maker, watching films some adults thought we shouldn't be and binge drinking, I ensured my various discomforts continued. After early mass, I threw up. I'd been very drunk the night before. Four years later in Sydney I left the church and the Church for the last time – 'You'll never be happy' – ringing in my ears– and made my way up to Oxford Street looking for Capriccios.

I still have a minor interest in Newman. He eventually became a Cardinal. I admired him for a time for voting no to Papal Infallibility at the First Vatican Council, 1869–1870, until I discovered he did so only because of misgivings about the potential overreach made possible by the wording of the relevant motion rather than disbelief in its core. I have visited the Brompton Oratory in London, a spin-off from the oratory founded by Newman in Birmingham. Brompton Oratory is a bastion of conservative Catholicism with a large congregation. Mass is said every day in Latin, as well as English. There is no place for progressive theology or social reform.

I spoke about Newman briefly at the second Homosexual Histories conference in Melbourne in 1999.

Lytton Strachey in his *Eminent Victorians* (1918) sardonically locates the moment of Newman's conversion in the agitation caused by 'the indiscreet activity of one of his proselytes.' In effect, Strachey said, Newman was sent silly by a young opera queen and went for incense, capes and bells as fast as he could.

The only overtly Christian artefact in my house is a small, hinged Byzantine wooden diptych. It is, of course, a reproduction. The stamped piece of paper headed 'certificate' on the back claims in English, French, German and Italian that it is a handmade copy of an old Byzantine icon. The tourist trade looms large in the certification, however the figures themselves seem consistent with Byzantine iconography. Holy figures on horseback grace both panels, facing each other on a golden background. I thought I knew who gave the diptych to me, but it seems I may be wrong. Be that as it may, it was a gift of an unexpected kind which pleased me. Its rich colours are redolent of other times and places of which I know little. Splendid archaic reds and blues are interwoven with gold accoutrements. The horses are prancing. The riders are defenders of a faith not so much long gone as distant, and mysterious. I write 'the only overtly Christian artefact', but there are also several large and small Christmas snowdomes mostly given to me by Leigh that I bring out annually for seasonal decorative purposes.

I consult Dino on the diptych. He tells me the writing on each of the two hinged panels is ecclesiastical Greek. The artist is Arsenios Irskios.

St Georgios/George is on the left panel and St. Demetrios is on the right. Both are warriors. Magnified inspection shows that St Georgios' spear is deep in a prostrate dragon's mouth. St Georgios is reputed to be a Greek who became a Roman soldier. Bugger me, and I thought he was English. He is after all their patron saint, but my assumption had begun to unravel some years ago when I saw statues of George and the dragon in Lutheran churches in Stockholm and Berlin. Demetrios' spear holds a soldier to the ground.

The pressure for a second cabinet grows. The diptych is one of several small works of art, also gifts, each of which deserves a shelf of its own.

The nineteenth century English aesthete Walter Pater wrote about Leonardo da Vinci's painting the Mona Lisa in a fantastically sweeping passage owing much to German romanticism ('modern philosophy') and English Hellenism, with a moment of camp – 'Lady Lisa'. The face of beauty – woman as goddess – is generalised across millennia. She is 'older than the rocks on which she sits', made emblematic of all human experience. It is a beauty 'wrought out from within upon the flesh'. The corporeal body is but a shell for the spiritual. The face is beacon and mirror: 'what in the ways of a thousand years men had come to desire'. A secular Mary emerges, Mona, whose job is much the same. Pater wrote this in 1868 in a search for a transcendental value to replace the failure of Christianity.

Aesthetics, in this version, became part of a homosexuality made publicly visible almost thirty years later in the first of two trials of Oscar Wilde for acts of gross indecency. Wilde was involved in three trials. In the first he was a prosecution witness when he sued the Marquis of Queensbury for libel. In the next two, Wilde himself was the accused.

He spoke from the dock of male love in his own Platonic defence of homosexuality in much the same idealised terms. It is one of the most powerful defences of male homosexuality in public history. Nothing was heard of blood, sweat or semen. There were, however, tears, during and after. In the circumstances, tactically, it couldn't be otherwise. As it was, the first trial was aborted. 'The love that dare not speak its name' had been spoken. A further trial ensued. He went to prison.

Chairman Mao said words to the effect of bend with the wind, but do not break.

It is sage advice that I have often used to temper my personal responses during difficult times, but it has its limits. Of perhaps 85,000 people who began the long march in the 1934 retreat from the Nationalist forces during the Chinese civil war, maybe 8000 were alive at its finish a year later. Enemy attack, starvation and cold take away the capacity to bend.

I come back to objects associated with those in the china cabinet, and the cabinet itself. It is more a glass display case than a piece of notable furniture. The only wood to be seen is at the top and bottom. Square wooden boards hold the almost invisible struts in place. They in turn support the three glass shelves on which the china sits. It is a transparent structure. The objects seem to be almost floating in air. The optics of display trump the closed doors of storage.

I am imagining that one day soon there may be laser cabinets with virtually displayed objects that one accesses from a visual equivalent of Spotify or the like. I look forward to it. That way I might get some Clarice Cliff china or a piece by Rene Lalique. I think of his corsage ornament 'Dragonfly Woman', and its exquisitely designed rendering in precious stones. Fine art merges with the decorative.

Champagne tastes and beer pockets, some might still say, but I do not mind just looking.

Clarice Cliff's work, of which I have none, is quite well known. She popularised modernist tableware. It is possible her brightly coloured, innovative designs influenced Woolworths' china range in the 1930s and according to journalist and publisher Stewart Dalby Woolworths at one point stocked her work.

Cliff was born and worked in Stoke-on-Trent, a town of pits and potteries in Staffordshire, England. Marian Pitts tells me Stoke was and is a collection of six towns that had grown up around the pits and became known for the potteries that relied on coal and local clay for production. These were brokered relations between production, design and trade. The Woolworths museum website tells us that the Woolworths buyers had links with the Staffordshire potteries and kept an eye out for new styles and designs. New items were then given a try-out. This kept the buyers in touch with changing customer preferences. Once a winner was identified the Buyer had two weeks to place an order for all the stores in Britain and Ireland.

By the 1970s, Cliff's work had become 'collectible'. Christies' 1983 auction of her pottery attracted buyers from all over the UK and the USA. The work was simultaneously seen as 'art pottery' fit for museums and galleries and as antique collectibles. Leonard Griffin asks in *Clarice Cliff The Bizarre Affair* (1988) why was it that factory produced primarily functional pottery became so collectible. Part of the answer lies in the sheer quantity of her production, accompanied by the considerable variety evident in the designs. The variety occurred between patterns and within them. For example, the Applique range eventually had fourteen patterns after starting with two. The china was available by mail order and in shops and was often exciting if not dramatic. Another part of the answer is in the quality of the design. A new relationship was established between the angularity of the visual design, the shape of the objects, the colour choices and the use of freehand decoration. One didn't just buy a piece of china, one bought a brand (Cliff), a patterned range (*Bizarre*, *Fantasque*, *Delecia*, *Appliqué*) a specific design. The buyer gained access to modernity.

The 'Cliff' brand became possible when Cliff's signature was eventually included on her designs. According to her biographer Lynn Knight, Cliff was not the first woman for whom this had happened, but the popularity of her designs appears to have been instrumental in breaking the tradition of anonymity in a design and decoration workforce that was largely female. By 1970, Wedgewood owned the potteries.

Another stream of popularising interest was also at work in the 1970s and after. Feminists identified, recuperated, celebrated the work of female artists, writers, ceramicists, designers. People collect for multiple reasons. The reasons aggregate and intersect. A trend emerges and becomes a boom.

Cliff created this intersection between brand and design as a ceramics designer in the 1920s and 1930s. It is a process repeated over and over in other arenas. Warhol's 1986/1987 unfinished car series for Mercedes Benz is another example: two brands (Warhol and MB) mesh in silk-screened acrylic on canvas. Cars become art and the name of Warhol sells it.

In a 1963 essay for *Esquire* magazine, Tom Wolfe celebrated customised cars as fetishized objects in what became a defining moment of 'new journalism'. His rapid-fire stylistics grabbed attention with a stream of lively first-person observations on customs, styles, designs, people – a specific car culture, its fans, their behaviour. The essay later introduced a book of essays, *The Kandy-Kolored Tangerine-Flake Streamline Baby* (1965). Tangerine? What madness is that? Whose fast lane tastes were these?

The teenagers involved, Wolfe said, were 'slaves to form.' He also speaks of Beau Brummel wearing 'one perfect starched cravat.' This is a long way from formalist theories of art, though there is an eye for virtuoso starching.

The Russian literary formalist Viktor Shklovsky wrote in 1925 about renewing perception through technical innovation ('making strange'). While aesthetic innovation shocks, or irritates some, that newness of design is what also makes some objects and practices desirable. For me it became a doorway to thinking differently, renewing and reinforcing my engagement with continental intellectual traditions. Now I would insist minimally that the physicality of the object is itself also important, especially if has deviated materially from the familiar and requires new forms of production: a triangular handle can be a visual surprise, a delight, but also uncomfortable if not impractical to use. What 'sells' it and to whom? Is my materialism too vulgar? Not, I would suggest, if we include in such a discussion examples of the social and aesthetic pushing and pulling involved in, say, the emergence of art deco (the decorative arts) in various contexts: commercial visual design, fashion and advertising, domestic china, metal work, furniture making, jewellery, architecture, and haute couture. Art Deco design criss-crosses the borders between commercial and industrial arts, *objet d'art* and less frequently fine art – *objet de vertu*, such as ornate Faberge eggs.

German *Jugendstil*, roughly the same period as French Art Nouveau, went for functionalism and clean lines, more often orienting itself to department stores and industrial manufacturing. We can see these aspects culminating in the work of the Bauhaus. French Art Deco revivified 'style' relying heavily on precious metals, veneers from wood that came from their colonies, and desires in the 'roaring twenties' for the high life. Style is linked to national pride and disdain, to 'success', to taste and discrimination. These rivalries were played out over and over.

But the twenties are also the Jazz Age: rowdy, lively, ear inspiring. It's the time of the Harlem Renaissance, radio, the phonograph and the speakeasies that emerged in the face of prohibition: the Cotton Club, Duke Ellington and the revival of the Klu Klux Klan.

These too are memorable across decades.

Billie Holiday first sang and recorded 'Strange Fruit' in 1939. The 'fruit' are the bodies of lynched African Americans. It was written by a Jewish New Yorker, then-communist Abel Meeropol, first as a poem in 1936 and then as a song in 1937. It has been sung frequently ever since: Nina Simone, UB40, Diana Ross, Jeff Buckley, Annie Lennox ...

Writing too was and is at stake in these discussions, as was homosexuality in the Harlem Renaissance in New York. Like Isaac Julien, the black British filmmaker who made a lyrical homage to the artists of that movement in *Looking for Langston* (1989), 'I am interested in poetry.' Leigh introduced me to Isaac's work and Isaac himself in 1987 when Isaac visited Sydney. The three of us met again in London early the following year. He was a fan of Derek Jarman's films especially at that time *Caravaggio* (1986).

A week or two after Leigh and I landed in London James Baldwin died: December 1, 1987. I was rocked. I had read most of his novels and many of his essays after reading Altman's *Homosexual*. His angry but considered engagement with religion in *Go Tell it on the Mountain* resonated with me, though I knew almost nothing of black American Pentecostalism. (Baldwin was a Pentacostal preacher at fourteen.) After Leigh left London for Australia, I went off to the University of Aarhus in Denmark to deliver a seminar paper at the invitation of Professor Anna Rutherford (1932–2001). Anna directed the Commonwealth Literature Centre there. Anna and I had met at the 1985 annual conference of the Association for the Study of Australian Literature in Armadale where I gave perhaps the first openly gay and lesbian paper on Rosa Praed's novel *Affinities* (1886). Oscar appears thinly disguised as one of her characters. At that conference, I mispronounced the name of another character, Colquhoun, as it is spelled. Someone later quietly and considerately told me that it is pronounced Calhoun. You can take the boy out of Bandiana, but ...

I returned to London from Denmark to find that Raymond Williams had died. He was a cultural materialist and a founding figure in Cultural Studies. He explored the relations between what people do in everyday life, cultural forms and wider social forces. Williams changed the way I thought, as did Baldwin.

One Saturday in 2017 Leigh turned up for lunch at Marios in Brunswick St. Fitzroy, and gave me a second-hand copy of a first edition of Williams' *The Long Revolution* (1961). He had found it in an op shop. The front page had '$10 UK Hist' pencilled on it. Tilting the book towards the light I also saw a faint embossed raised notation:

Leeds University Union Library. I think of the thoughtfulness embodied in that seemingly simple action, embedded as it is in our mutual history, and my delight in receiving the book. Like cups and designs, books and affection circulate in all sorts of ways.

Williams died in Saffron Walden, Essex. Coincidentally Liz and her daughter Katherine were staying there in 2016 while Katherine gave a paper at Cambridge as part of her work for a PhD. I often stay with Liz in Marrickville when I am in Sydney. We try and meet when she is in Melbourne, and mostly do. I met her at Sydney University in 1973 at the time of the Philosophy strike. Our friendship grew after I returned to Sydney in 1985. I have known Kath since she was a baby in Redfern and Newtown. I went up to Saffron Walden from London for a couple of nights and Liz and I went from there on a day trip to gawp at Ely Cathedral. It is constructed on an extraordinary scale. Its centrepiece is an octagonal tower built after the original Norman tower collapsed. My father once joked that he went to Cambridge. He did: Cambridge Tech.

Mine are practised gestures, flourishes, crafted poses, shifts in the flow of things. What more, after all, can the writing of life be? I practise practices. I have a taste for composition.

In 1996, the poet Pam Brown wrote in her poem 'Ol' Shallow Throat',

> all *my* favourite
> breezy modernists,
> O'Hara, Elmslie,
> Denby, Schuyler,
> Ashbery   et al.,
> were & are
> poofs,

& half
the Beats to boot—
...
dropsical old bods
now   blowing
gummy sucky kisses
to the latest,   the
loveliest,
the shallowest, to
square old putti
just like me

My initial thought was I'd much rather be a
dropsical old bod than a square old putto, but
hey, either way, I'm the one writing about teapots,
and yes, of course, I can be both. In ancient Greek
culture putti were winged, pudgy, childlike, secular
beings who influenced human affairs. In the
Baroque period (1600–1750) they were represented
as cherubs/cherubim and appeared as little angels.
And yes, I too am ageing – 'old'. Dropsy is a medical
condition involving the accumulation of watery
fluids under the skin. (Play with it. De-medicalise
it. Smirk even.) As it is, but not because of dropsy,
when I fly I wear a pressure stocking on my right leg.
It still swells, but perhaps not as much as it might
do without the stocking. I contact Pam who tells me
that one of the narrators of the poem, 'Ol' Shallow
Throat' himself, is uneasy with homosexuality –
'he's "progressive" and homophobic.' The text gags
with and at and in that space of contradiction partly
through the introduction of an *italicised* second
narrator/commentator:

Certain   almost special
homosexuals & lesbians
are tolerable   even
acceptable   definitely

77

     marketable   (*ta*
     to the heavens
     for <u>*that*</u>*, sweetie*)

There is no truck from Ol' Throaty's point of view
with the notion that surface can be as telling as depth.
    I like to think that I am engaged here in this
writing of life in what Australian cultural studies
scholar Professor Meaghan Morris once called in
a different context, 'sociable disjunction'. That is,
I put unexpected things together in what is meant
to be a productive way, rather than simply putting
them in opposition to each other. In writing life
as I do here, psychology has a limited place, and
though there are deliberate autobiographical traces,
tracks, I did not set out initially to write as I have.
The form happened as I wrote, and as it flowed and
as I became aware of what I was doing narrative
interruption was naturalised, made ordinary. I am
surprised, distracted, by myself.
    Writing, for me, is exactly that, an everyday
day cultural practice, even as I acknowledge
that is not consciously the case for many people
and literacy is not available to all, but Raymond
Williams long ago took on the implications of
mass literacy and its effects: 'culture is ordinary'.
He refused to sharply separate culture and
society while acknowledging that in certain ways
of thinking this is what had occurred. On the
surface, speaking of culture as everyday life is a
simple statement, but historically, as Williams
showed in *The Long Revolution* mass print literacy
amongst other things is a democratising process
with profound social and political implications.
Language, as Barthes put it, forces one to speak,
however much one modulates it for tone or
situational appropriateness or is selectively silent.
Literacy changed shape radically again with the

arrival of photography, film, radio, television, the internet and mobile phones: mass communication and virtual reality.

Ordinary culture, the everyday, includes the spectacular, the shocking, novelty, the flicker, the shake, the designed, the unintended, the banal and the regular.

These techno-affective developments of various kinds change the ways we think, see, hear and yes, feel. They distribute cultural capital differently, create resistances, excite new socialities, entertain, educate; scramble our radar, confuse our bearings; charm, harm, deliver, produce. They do so globally in the footsteps of imperialism – globalisation. Too determinist for you? Let's talk later, but not till we consider the current international refugee crises and the various extremities of response their desperation incites.

In September 2001, I left New York for Melbourne a few days before 9/11. Craig rang me at 7am to tell me what had happened and to turn on my television. I saw endless footage of the towers collapsing. 3000 dead. (It had occurred late in the night, Australian time.) You didn't have to know a lot to know the response would be as disastrous as the terrorist acts that caused it. We have lived with the consequences of both ever since. 'You can't blow up a social relationship.' Unless, of course, you decimate populations and raze villages, towns and cities.

Meaghan made her remark about 'sociable disjunction' in an analysis amongst other things of a John Forbes poem, 'Watching the Treasurer' – at that time (1983–1991) Paul Keating, who shortly after became Prime Minister of Australia. He was seen by his fans in the press as 'street smart' and a 'high flyer', a combination that 'resolved' class tensions.

He could mesmerise the camera with those great big burning brown eyes, then move in with a stream of jargon which seemed on the surface unintelligible and yet which let you know, quite simply and profoundly, that really everything would be all right if you just *suffered* a little more, and let him take care of business.

Fascination and anxiety. Both those who were unemployed at the time and those of us paying 17% interest on our mortgages were also anxious. She valued Forbes' poems, she said, because they gave her ideas, ways of thinking through what was happening. Her interest was in the Australian media's "infatuation" with Keating. 'Watching the Treasurer' begins,

> I want to believe the beautiful lies
> the past spreads out like a feast.
>
> Television is full of them & inside
> their beauty you can act

'Inside their beauty you can act': we are immersed in the realm of media spectacle. It is a discussion in part about ideology. Who can act? How? Who benefits? I move straight to Guy Debord: 'All that once was directly lived has become mere representation.' If that is so, and I have not missed some irony, then representation cannot be considered as 'mere'. It matters. Sociality is mediated through the communication circuits of media narration. I find the notion that anyone has lived 'directly', without mediation, more than slightly weird. Kirsty Machon tells me there may be translation issues here with 'mere'. It can be translated in different ways – 'moved away into a representation' – but my remark still stands.

All lives are lived in social contexts, but except when forgotten that is almost a dismissible given, a starting point. I say 'almost' in order to acknowledge that this is part of an argument that went on for most of the twentieth century in discussions of aesthetics and politics, as well as in constructions of 'true' selves that ignore the social in socialisation and identity formation. Some of the aesthetic and politics discussion occurred in the name of style and form and the power and the limits of representation and interpretation as ways of understanding things. In a way this is all beside the point. Debord wanted to shake 'modern passivity' by disintegrating spectacle.

David Halperin quotes Oscar Wilde on these surfacing matters in *How to be Gay*: 'The true mystery of the world is the visible.' Halperin then speaks of what it was Susan Sontag was doing in *Against Interpretation* and her 'Notes on "Camp"'.

> Instead of ...interpretation, a quest to discover what a work of art deeply, truly means, she urged us to take on an erotics of art, an appreciation of surfaces, a description of aesthetic values, of style and its effects ... what she was really describing in 'Notes on "Camp"' was a style of relation to various cultural objects.

Style, for Halperin, is 'a deviation from a norm'. What is needed is an interpretation of surfaces. Style, he says, has its own content.

In 1982, I was staying for a few months with Paul Rubner in Glebe. Paul had introduced me to Debord's ideas, and those of the Situationists, in the mid-1970s. I would not claim to have 'got' situationism then, nor now. From Paul's, I often walked to visit Jan McKemmish in Mary St, Glebe.

There we continued what became a twenty-five-year conversation about the poetics and politics of representation, the nature of language, of writing and figures of speech. In the meantime, Jan worked on her first novel *A Gap in the Records*, published by Sybylla Co-Operative Press to critical acclaim in 1985. Virginia had lived in the same block before heading off to London for the next twenty years. In the next flat over from Jan's, Gillian Leahy was directing the making of *My Life Without Steve* (1986). It won major awards at both the Melbourne and Sydney film festivals. More recently Gill had considerable success with the award-winning *Baxter and Me* (2016). Jan was a journalist for a while on *Tribune*, and in 1990 invited me to write an obituary for Patrick White. I wrote it at Ken Charnock's house in Penrith. He was very ill, but still working and urging me on. Jan went on to teach writing at UTS and in the mid 1990s was invited by John Frow to set up the graduate creative writing programme at the University of Queensland. She died in Melbourne on Christmas Eve, 2007.

> It is a saxophone before dawn time.
> It is blue music on a black night ...
> It's the moment before a story begins ...
> Spiders talk in whispers.
> The moment of illumination. Dawn.
> > (Jan McKemmish, *A Gap in the Records*)

Those who can, teach.

Jan and Pam Brown were friends and sometime collaborators. They each appeared in Sybylla Press's 1982 anthology, *Frictions*, edited by Anna Gibbs and Alison Tilson. One of their 'Generic Ghost' collaborations was the intertextual performance piece 'As Much Trouble as Talking'. It was directed by Helen Grace and performed at the Belvoir Theatre in August 1988. This was followed by a joint playwriting residency at the Performance Space in 1989.

Quotes shaped and reshaped each other, experimentally, playfully, wittily, humorously; juxtaposition turned discontinuity and interruption into an exploration of new possibilities for feminist politics and poetics.

I met Jan through Virginia in the mid-seventies in Melbourne. I had met Virginia some months earlier in Sydney. I shared a house with Gill and others in 1975 and met Virginia there after a group came back from a feminist conference in Canberra. I moved to Melbourne for the first time later that year after I in turn had attended the first national homosexual conference there in August. Craig Johnston delivered a paper he and I had written together for the conference at his suggestion – 'Campfires of the Resistance'. Craig's 1999 book *A Sydney Gaze* collected his major pieces on the politics of Gay Liberation and its re-formation into a 'gay movement' and 'community' politics. Graham Willett in his review of the book in *Arena* wrote: 'It is Johnston's gift to be able to see more clearly than most where we are at – and what comes next.'

Jan was then a teacher in Brunswick. The three of us along with Di Wilson had a picnic drink in Royal Park and listened to Linda Ronstadt and Jackson Brown on, I guess, a cassette player. Jan loved crisply ironed white cotton sheets, good coffee and a fine cheese complemented by equally fine writing. It was not until decades later that I knew about the sheets. Gill had introduced me to Pam in Glebe in 1975. We very briefly visited Pam to get a copy of her second publication *Cocabola's Funny Picture Book* (1974), however it was the mid

1980s before Pam and I began to crossover more frequently, often at readings, conferences and parties. One of the things I share with Pam is having had over forty addresses though I suspect she is ahead of me now. We each had army fathers and had separately arrived in Sydney in 1968. Jan and Pam both liked tea and talk as many of us do. It was often accompanied by lively rumination. She and Pam were friends for thirty-one years.

They made and mined an archive of textual forms and manoeuvres. They performed it as an archive of present possibilities.

Or as art historian Rosalind Krauss might have put it, I was introduced to a paraliterary focus on narrative strategies and the primacy of the surface.

After winning the Adelaide Festival Award for Poetry in 2018, Pam was awarded the Australian Literary Society Gold Medal in 2019.

I read the narrator in Pam's poem as more than a little bit envious, if not resentfully mocking, of those who enjoy passing notoriety. Warhol's fifteen minutes.

> Just like
> the 19th Century
> (oh, _everybody_
> _shops there_
> _these days)_
> these softening brutes
> squabbling
> & helplessly fractious
> as the appalling night
> closes

He condescends to offer to 'the softening brutes' 'my continuing/acquaintance'. Read now, twenty years later, the voice of that narrator is at least momentarily resurgent. It evokes Prime Minister

Turnbull attending Sydney's Gay and Lesbian Mardi Gras in 2016, his subsequent failures in relation to marriage equality and the resulting disputes when the Mardi Gras board wanted to invite him again for 2017. There is more to this than 'squabble'. Moralist conservatism often downplays what is at stake for those most affected.

On the third shelf down in my cabinet are two grey and white Christian Lacroix coffee cups and saucers that Craig gave me for my fiftieth in 1999. They are described as a 'Follement (Gold Trim) Flat Demitasse Cup and Saucer Set.' Edina from *Ab Fab* would be proud of both of us. I still have the box they came in. 'Follement' translates as wildly, madly. It is a formal conceit. They are elegant with a touch of frivolity. The decoration borders the area where the handle attaches. A thin gold line of upwardly curving scrolling separates the grey and white. Craig and I both lived in Darlinghurst at the time. We had met at Sydney University in 1973, shared a house with others in Annandale in 1974, overlapped in Melbourne for a year in 1977, travelled for a while together with Robert Johnston in 1988, and chanted in Haymarket at some later point during his lunch hour. We kept in touch, still do. Several of us from those university days stay in contact, sometimes frequently, sometimes with long gaps in between. As with many people's long-term friendships, the connection is immediate as soon as we are together again.

In 2016, I received a postcard from Craig sent while he was in Sri Lanka. He likes to send postcards as do Leigh and Graham, even though we also email and message when travelling. The card Craig sent is a reproduction of Victor J Trip's poster from the 1950s: 'Ceylon The Home of Good Tea'. It can be found in the state-owned gift and souvenir boutique, Laksala, in Columbo. The image is familiar. An anonymous muscular male drummer, bare chested in a shadowy green, occupies most of the frame on a fawn background. In the front is an anonymous woman on a much smaller scale picking leaves from a tea bush. The image is stylish and has been included in the Stick No Bills™ Vintage Tea Posters of Ceylon series. Exotica and vague erotica displace colonial economic relations. Many of the workers on the tea plantations were Tamils imported from India by British planters in the nineteenth century. Much of the tea was picked by women. The Tamils were dirt poor and disenfranchised. Ceylon declared independence from British rule in 1948 and became a republic named Sri Lanka in 1972. (It had also been colonised before the British by the Portuguese and the Dutch.) The individuals within the image become generic 'people of Ceylon'. This in turn makes for a generic picturesqueness intended to be generative of touristic desire. That's not why Craig was there. He had quite specific purposes, but it is not for me to identify them here.

I passed through the port of Colombo with my parents on a boat full of ten pound-a-head poms in early 1952. Somewhere on that six week trip to Australia I had whooping cough. As the boat continued on from Fremantle to Sydney the trip must have seemed interminable. We stayed in Sydney a few months at my mother's Great Aunt's, before the army posted my father to the Army Apprentices School at Balcombe Army Camp in Mount Martha, about sixty kilometres south of Melbourne. Balcombe was established in 1939 as a training camp for soldiers in WW II. The school for apprentices came after the war. These are retrospective stories of empires, and their effects. Trip, the painter of the original Ceylon poster, was born in 1913 to Dutch parents in Batavia

(Jakarta) then known as the Dutch East Indies and interned by the Japanese during WWII. He died in Rotterdam in 1975. Colonialism, militarism, war, and the shaping of lives.

On the bottom shelf are two sets of Myott 'English Countryside' cups, saucers, small plates and a sturdy milk jug. These were given to me by Jan Hutchinson on my fortieth birthday at the Glebe Rowing Club in 1989. Jan made the cake of piled profiteroles bound by a chocolate sauce. We danced to a live band led by Peter Doyle.

I had seen and admired Jan H's Myott china many times in her house in Annandale where she lived with her son Ben. Myott was also a Staffordshire pottery from another of the six towns, Hanley. Their pieces are neither signed nor dated. The ones Jan gave me are 'English Countryside'. A yellowish scalloped base is ringed ('trimmed') with gold. There is a decorative band featuring Tudor style, thatch roofed houses. The thatch is a high gloss black. On either side of the double gabled house there is a small copse of three trees. Each tree has a brown trunk and inverted umbrella branches at their tops point upwards. The sky is cloudy, and the centre of the plate and the bottom half of the cups are bare. Jan knew I liked them.

There we have it: a teapot, four sets of cups, saucers and sometimes plates, an ashtray and a key ring.

Jan H. and I had met in 1982 through a mutual friend, Graham Templeman, when I was in Sydney for several months, but it was not until the later 1980s that we grew closer. In early 1985, after completing a master's degree, I had left Melbourne for a lectureship at the then NSW Institute of Technology (NSWIT). Shortly after, it became the University of Technology, Sydney (UTS). In 1986 Jan had enrolled in a Graduate Diploma in

Writing. She sat in front of me the first year I taught the introductory subject 'Word and Text' in the BA in Communications. In 1989, McPhee Gribble published Jan's collection of stories, *Desire and Other Domestic Problems*. She invited me to speak at the launch at the Harold Park Hotel in Glebe which had regular writing nights – 'Writers in the Park'. I did it with a degree of cheek, if not effrontery. I rewrote her story 'Waiting for the Garbos' about a man and a woman in bed woken by the garbage collectors. I called mine 'Working for the Garbos', pinched her characters and made the man in hers bi and my garbo gay.

Some months later Jan produced a third story in which she in turn took one of my characters and killed him off. We began reading them to the UTS Writers Group and occasionally at the Harold Park, and developed a small following. Three more stories followed. Stephen Muecke, then the publisher of Local Consumption Publications, and an academic colleague, asked if we would like to publish them. We did, in 1991, in a jointly authored book of fiction and essays called *Two Timing. Sex, writing and the writing of sex*. It was launched by Liz and Leigh. Leigh had edited it. Patrick McIntyre, a student at the time, reviewed it and referred to its 'gorgeous melancholy'. I had to think about that. I still do.

I have sometimes been asked to speak at the launch of other people's books, resources and monographs. After Jan's book launch came Lynne Segal's *Slow Motion. Changing masculinities, changing men*, at Gleebooks in Sydney in1991. Another was Kirsty Machon's short story collection, *Immortality*, published by Blackwattle Press, in 1996.

Kirsty's and my trajectories have criss-crossed over the past twenty years and more. We both now live in Melbourne, coincidently currently in the same suburb. In the 1990s we were each separately closely associated with national HIV/AIDS organisations. Kirsty was a sometime editor of *Positive Living* and the *National AIDS Bulletin*, each of which I occasionally wrote for. She became the Health and Treatments Policy Officer for the National Association of People Living with HIV/AIDS (NAPWA) and represented the organisation on various research committees, including the International Network for Strategic Initiatives in Global HIV Trials and the Consumers Health Forum. Over the last ten years or so we have met intermittently for coffee. We caught up in London in 2016 and explored the church of St Bartholomew the Great, half of which was demolished in 1543 during the dissolution of the monasteries. That's the lawn bit before you walk in the now main door. A small tour of St Bart's Hospital followed, where we looked at Hogarth paintings on the Great Hogarth Stairway. Kirsty was by then finishing her PhD on evolutionary philosophy. We wandered off to Tower Bridge and enjoyed the sun while she filled me in on Darwin and Thomas Henry Huxley.

I was unsure initially about what to say when launching *Slow Motion*. In hindsight I doubt I had ever launched a book before and Gleebooks had an aura of its own. I consulted Jan H. She suggested I start with Merv Hughes. I looked at her blankly and she had to remind me he was a cricketer who kissed other players on the field when he did something good. Scandalous! I was reminded of the front-page poster of Prince Andrew pinned to the notice board of the Harold Park Hotel. It said, 'They call me Mavis.'

Slow Motion mattered to me because it refused simplistic arguments that denied or ignored the evidence of differences amongst men and amongst women. Lynne's intellectual and political framework allowed for a politics of change in the social and economic relations between women and men. She recognized and described where change was occurring without minimizing the difficulties involved. She saw the linkages between misogyny and homophobia, between sex, gender and racism but kept open the possibilities for ongoing, if not large-scale, social change.

I no longer accept critiques that refuse to acknowledge how objectification and varieties of micro-power are frequently intrinsic to erotic attraction. Indeed they are often part of romance itself: the power of a look, a gesture, a looking away, a smile, a stare; the power of scent, of hair or hairlessness, of height, of muscle, of curves and hollows, of presence, the colour of eyes, a style of conversation, a way of laughing, a manner of being; whether choreographed or 'natural', all are constituents of attraction or otherwise, including the seduction of feeling at ease, sensing respect, mutual intellectual curiosity, or just being plain turned on. Acknowledging these matters does not automatically undercut the rejection of sexual violence or opposition to discriminatory inequalities. Nor does it intrinsically promote non-consenting behaviour. I think, for example, of more recent feminist work on sexual consent such as Kath Albury's *Yes Means Yes* (2002) and Moira Carmody's books on sexual ethics and young people. I was part of the launch of Moira's *Sex and Ethics: Young people and ethical sex* in 2009 at the State Library of NSW. Moira's work was about the negotiation of consent. She reconceptualised anti-rape education into programs for ethical erotics. One of the dimensions of care of the self, she wrote, was caring for others. Many years earlier she had been instrumental in setting up services for women who had been sexually assaulted and became central nationally in the development of anti-violence prevention strategies.

I start to remember how I thought about issues of power, objectification and sex changed. For me it came slowly until I eventually watched William Friedkin's *Cruising* some years after it was first released in 1980 and understood that its erotic edge both intrigued and excited me. Perhaps Al Pacino as a cop transmuting into a leather man had something to do with it. A serial killer is murdering gay men. Narrative tension does it for me. I had begun to face my own shyness and fears and associated sexual moralism. Ironically, that process also freed me to two-step with camp. My leather jacket became part of something more than a fashion statement, though I didn't take on a leather persona. Ken Charnock took me to the gym over Christmas 1986, and to the Paddington Green Hotel leather bar. I discovered the Den and saunas. This loosening-up played out in some of my fiction and ficto-criticism in the 1990s, but also in a much greater ease with, and acceptance of difference between, my personal cultural and sexual preferences and those of others.

Feminist friends were doing the same, at least one taking me by surprise with her delight in *Basic Instinct* (1992, Dir. Paul Verhoeven) and the erotic power of a strong woman. Others had already pointed me to the Sheba anthologies *Serious Pleasures* (1989) and *More*, yes, you guessed it, *Serious Pleasures* (1991). Joan Nestle and Pat Califia, later Patrick Califia-Rice, now Patrick Califia, amongst others broached the territory much earlier. Nestle reclaimed aspects of 1950s lesbian bar life, demanding lesbian feminism come to terms with butch and femme. In her *A Restricted Country* (1987) she wrote,

Although I have been a Lesbian for over twenty years and I embrace feminism as a world view, I can spot a butch thirty feet away and still feel the thrill of her power … this power is not bought at the expense of the femme's identity. Butch-femme relationships, as I experienced them, were complex erotic statements, not phony heterosexual replicas.

No post-Gutenberg book is a unique object as distinct from an individual one, unless cultural politics or personal preference declare it so. Some, however, are more distinctive in what they do than others.

In the back of my mind as I write around and through the objects in the china cabinet is Walter Benjamin's essay from 1936, 'The Work of Art in the Age of Mechanical Reproduction.' He spoke of how unique works of art are closely linked with tradition and of how tradition itself changes over time. Even so, he says, each period is confronted by the uniqueness of the object, its aura.

Individuality does not require or entail uniqueness. *Pace* Walter Benjamin, but these objects in my china cabinet, however more or less mass produced, still have an aura, at least for me. I acknowledge I am not using the word in quite the same way as in the original essay. Benjamin was marking out the difference between singular art objects that have been acclaimed by tradition and mass-produced objects. Mass production, he suggested, changed the processes of evaluation. I have no argument with that. The presence of the objects in the cabinet ensures their value. Each of them is a goodhearted gift. Each signifies a specific friendship with its own history – when we met, what developed, what continues, and how. Gifts sometimes bring obligation, invoke reciprocity, and occasionally produce rivalries of generosity.

Mostly, for me, however they mark out various degrees of fondness, intimacy, love and affection. They embody what mattered then and what matters now: mutualities. These bonds of intimacy –threads, strings, ties, links – have an importance different to that of the forms of the objects and their pleasures. The objects are things of beauty, but their significance is as much social and affective as aesthetic. As gifts, they materialise certain personal relations. Their authenticity, if indeed we have any need to go there at all, is not only a matter of that pristine moment when I saw the object for the first time and was delighted.

In his book *The Arcades Project* Benjamin wrote,

> Trace and aura. The trace is appearance of a nearness, however far removed the thing that left it behind may be. The aura is appearance of a distance, however close the thing that calls it forth. In the trace we gain possession of the thing; in the aura, it takes possession of us.

The friendship is not in the object, but in my relation to it, and its relation to other times and places. I received it. The object reminds, announces, declares, acknowledges giver and receiver. It is both relay station and totem.

That said, first sightings can have a magic. Do I remember that moment I first saw Michelangelo's David when I turned right into a corridor in the Galleria dell' Academia in Florence in 1988 and looked down a corridor and there he was? I do. Six tons of marble have a certain scale, especially when framed visually by a large archway. I was staggered by its power. Much of that came from position and height until I stood right before it and saw the sculpting of sinew, muscle, smoothness

and corrugation, the sheer physicality of thigh,
chest and face, big head, large hands. After all
the postcards, after all the pictures in art books,
after all the reverential speech and writing, it still
shone as though I had seen and heard nothing.
That memory remains. Right at that moment I
was alone in my wonder, despite the presence of a
few strangers doing much the same gawking, and
the knowledge that my two fellow travellers (Craig
and Robert) were nearby. Fancy says they were
possibly standing transfixed still in the nearby
Uffizi Gallery staring at Botticelli's Venus (another
delight). They weren't. I was simply ahead of them
as they lingered in the previous room. All this
awe after a hundred years or more of mechanical
reproductions that in a way had not prepared me.
They did tell me, or tried to, those traditions, what
I was supposed to like and respect. Benjamin was
right in that regard.

I note my automatic use of 'transfixed' and
indeed of 'aura'. Aura was a minor Titan god of
the breeze. The word aura became associated with
emanations and their associated atmospheres,
hence the 'aura' of a painting. Religiosity abounds,
particularly in romantic aesthetics. One is pierced
by awe at the sight of an object, instead of by a spear
on Calvary. Metaphor also abounds. One stands in
the light or hangs in it, in a gallery, on a hillside,
whatever the case may be. I also read, with what
reliability I don't know, that in Finnish 'aura' is a
popular type of blue cheese.

Benjamin was a Jewish Berliner who spent less
and less time in Germany after the Nazis burned
the German parliament in 1933. He fled Paris with
his sister the day before the Nazis arrived there in
1940 and six weeks later headed for Portugal with
a transit visa to the USA. Franco's police stopped
him in Portbou, Spain, and said the group he was

travelling with would be sent back to France. Both Benjamin and Arthur Koestler, who was also in the hotel, took overdoses. Benjamin died. Koestler survived to write *Darkness at Noon* (1940. Tr. 1941), set during the Stalinist purges and Moscow show trials of the late 1930s. What happened to Benjamin's sister? You may well ask. I tried to find out but have so far failed. His brother Georg died/ was killed/was murdered in the Mauthausen-Gusen concentration camp in 1942.

For all that, that mystique attached to 'original' singular works of art in Benjamin's essay, and his challenging of it, my four small shelves of objects, all mass produced, have their own significance. It is a modest claim. To reiterate, they matter to me because of their form and because they are gifts. They also force an ongoing, considered use of language. I am reminded of the comforts of friendship, of company, companionship, continuity, of reliability and trust, of sharp honesties and bitten tongues, of the weft and warp of intimacy, of Silvo and of not putting china with metallic finishes in the dishwasher.

I recall that after a long morning's discussion of texts, textuality and the writing of sentences with Jan McKemmish I thank her for our 'chat'. Who knew green brown eyes could flash? 'Chat, Michael, chat!' I had made a major category error. I hastened to substitute the word discussion for chat. I was being reminded of the hard work that goes into understanding writing and intellectual development, the very point of what we had been doing. Sometimes I do not bite my tongue enough. Leigh would laugh and say but that's what it is, chat. Indeed, he did just that.

Inevitably objects too can remind me also of the times I have produced exasperation in others, disappointed if not failed them. Loving someone does not always mean the relationship lasts. Objects can also bear witness to what was and what might have been still, to what broke or was broken. Over time, fine china can bear the lines and discolorations of careless use.

So, where does this get me, how far does it take me, this distinction between the social and the aesthetic, or more broadly, between the political, economic, social and cultural realms? And what happens when I am up against each of them simultaneously? What happens is a series of multiple explorations and valuations. Wonder and awe, delight, pleasure, a love of excess if not extremity, coexist with realism. A realism that in turn demands my respect for ordinary social connection that is not immediately defined by respectability or current social organisation of what pass as healthy minds. For what it is like to live with the resulting mess and muddle of making do and why we are so bothered by the lack of neatness that results. How do we wish to live with necessity and under what conditions?

I see I have moved from 'I' to 'we' in the preceding paragraph. The urge to make bigger claims is upon me. I step back. I speak (*darling*) between us though not in or with unqualified confidence. Textual intimacy is ever precarious. Come along with me please.

Out of sight in other cupboards are the Spode cup, saucer and plate Leonie gave me in 1984 when I left TAFE teaching in Melbourne and returned to Sydney. I had cut my teeth as a teacher first as a Philosophy tutor at the University of NSW in 1975, then as a teacher of night HSC English classes at University High School in Melbourne, 1977–1978. On the basis of this I gained entry to a graduate Dip. Ed. course and went on to teach English and Politics in the Tertiary Orientation Programme

96

at the then Caulfield Institute of Technology. For several years I was active in the Technical Teachers Union of Victoria, both in my local branch and the state committee structure. The first time I saw Bertolucci's 1900 was with Leonie's partner John Hird. The three of us were unionists. John and I also saw the 1984 film of le Carré's novel *The Little Drummer Girl* (Dir. George Roy Hill) together. Similar tastes in reading take you places. Both times we went to Camberwell, probably to the Rivoli.

The pieces Leonie gave me reproduce an 1838 blue, white and yellow floral pattern with fruit. Cahal Fairfield tells me the designs are examples of 'chinoiserie' from the late Regency period. The stylised, sophisticated pattern would have been thought to 'typify' Chinese culture. The rims are scalloped, and the sides of the cups are slightly fluted. The pattern is dated two years before the first opium war (1839–1842), a trade war between China and Britain which saw a decline in British interest in things Chinese. Nearby are two other Spode reproduction large tea cups with saucers, labelled 'Chinese Rose', dated 'c. 1815'. These cup rims are also scalloped with the barest hint of fluting. The flowers around the top half of the cups and saucers are tree blossoms in pinks, reds and blues. Each piece is numbered and stamped. They were also a gift and are reminders of a friendship that fell apart for reasons you do not need to know.

That said, those two friendships signified here by gifts of Spode mark out particular vectors of mutuality. Both involved aspects of mentorship and frequent companionship, mostly easy, sometimes not. Leonie taught me much about the pragmatics of teaching and the politics of active unionism, as well as opening me to opera and the making of a quick hearty soup to salve tired teachers in the after-work coldness of Melbourne's long winter nights. The unnamed friend often shared with me his working knowledge of styles of china. Pleasures come where they do. He also prompted – perhaps unwittingly – my now regular cooking of a turkey at Christmas. Neither friendship was sexual, but we knew each other intimately and affectionately. Both were tough-minded in ways I found salutary. They were social relationships formed in shared activities decades apart. Occasionally there are unexpected encounters or catch-ups that cross long periods of silence. The Spode speaks to me of these matters, bridges different times, force feeds memory simply by its presence when I open the cupboard door.

percussion
&
the *right* chords –
a little scat,
(no flatted fifths),
some clarinet,
a hot trumpet

(Pam Brown, 'West End Blues', *Missing Up*, 2015)

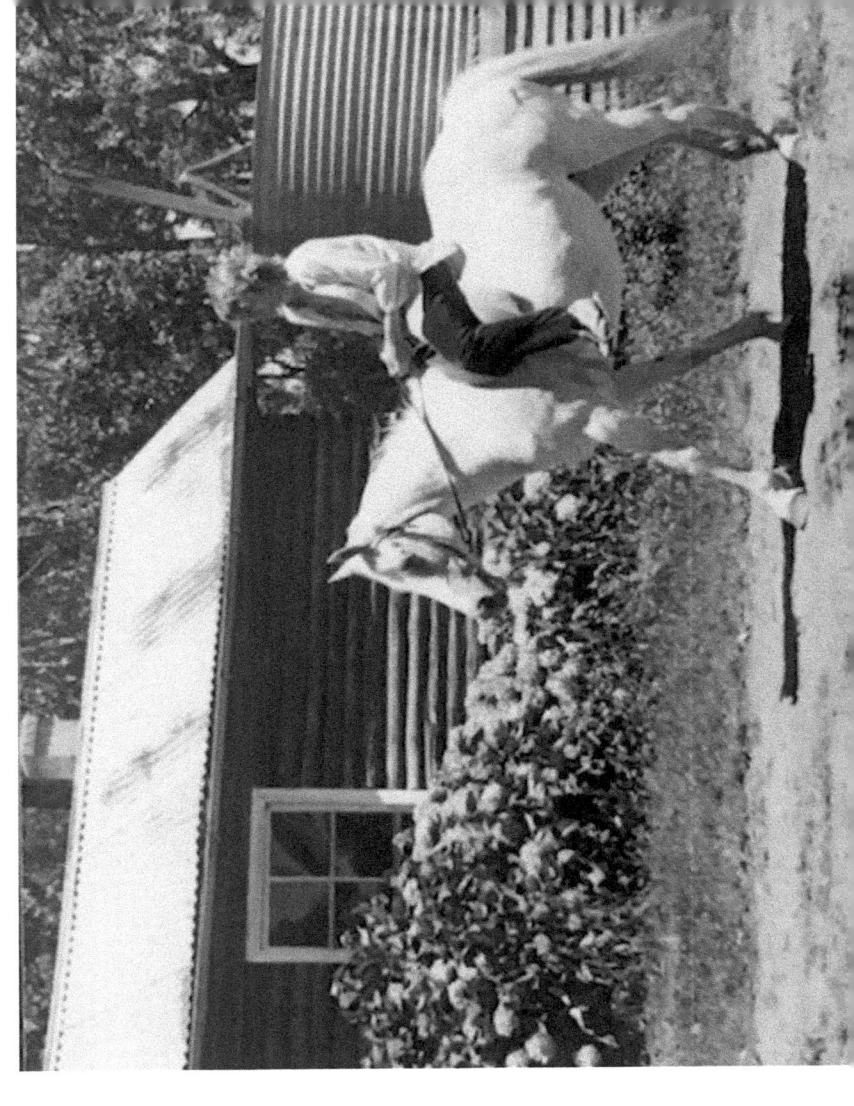

Michael Hurley,
Cockatoo, 1978.
Photographer:
Richard Riley

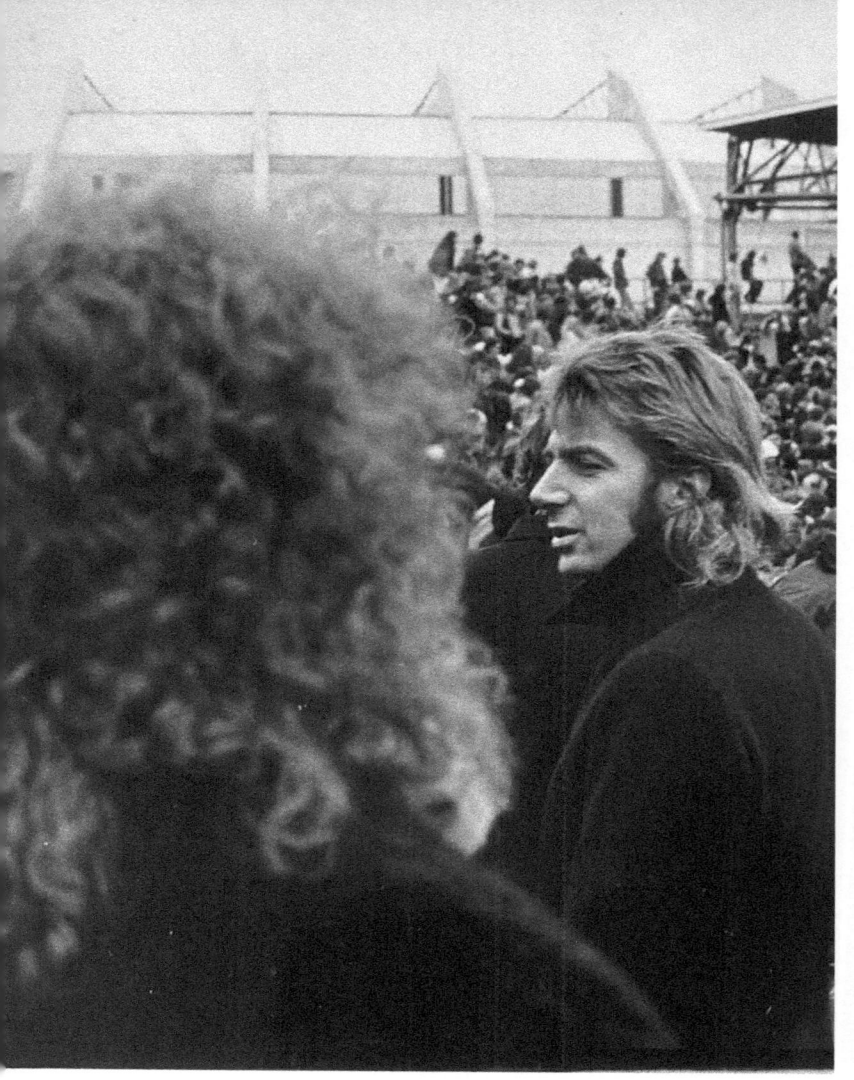

Michael Hurley, Melbourne Teachers' Strike, Richmond Oval, 1980. Photographer unknown.

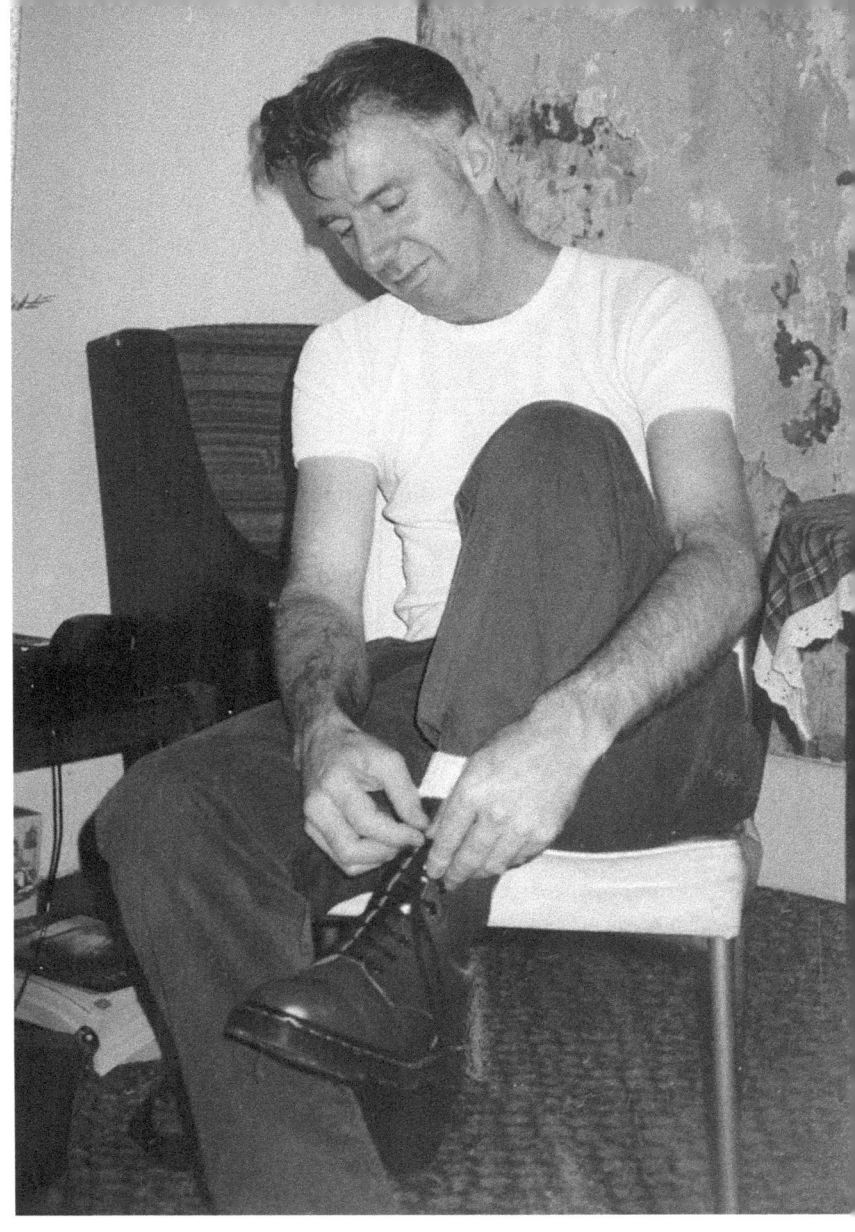

Michael Hurley, Camperdown, 1989. Photographer unknown.

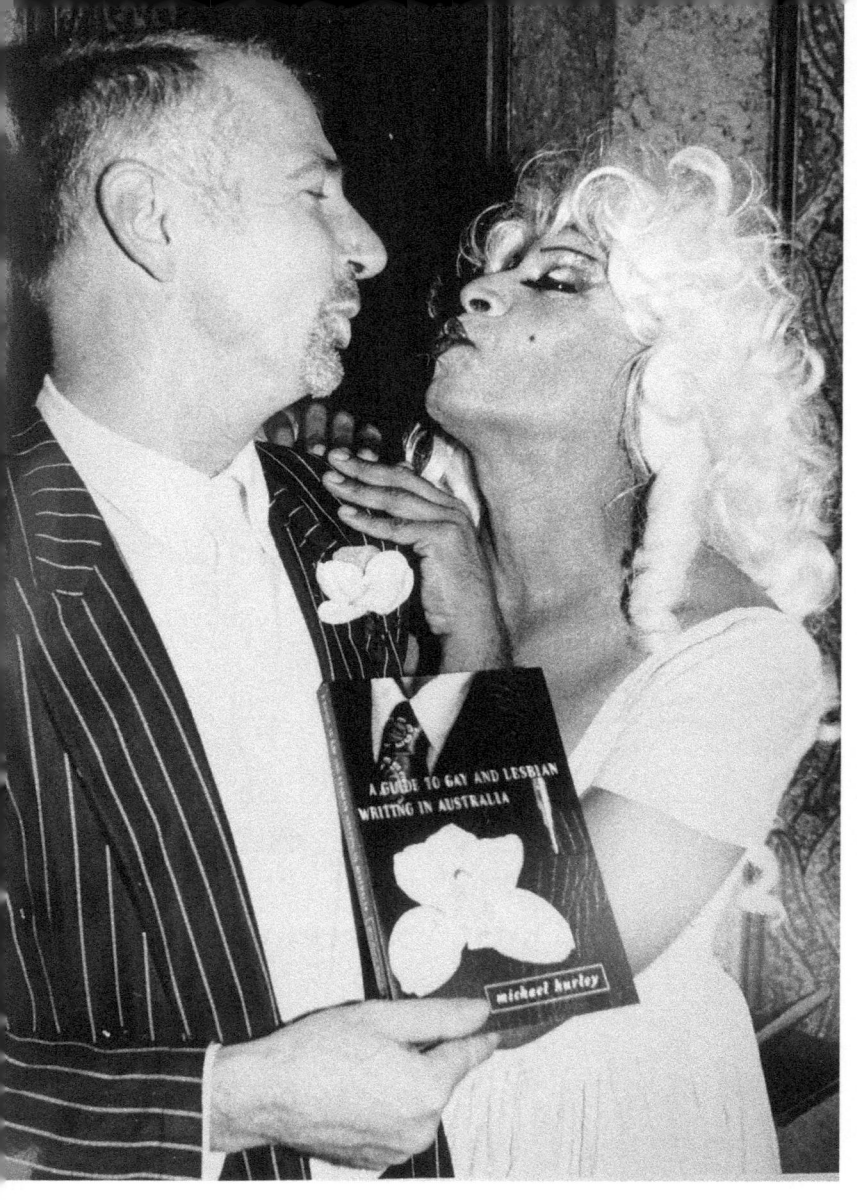

Michael Hurley, left, with Paul van Reyk aka Bonnie Beaucamp, State Theatre, Sydney, 1996, for the launch of Michael's book, *A Guide to Gay and Lesbian Writing in Australia*. Photographer: Mazz Image.

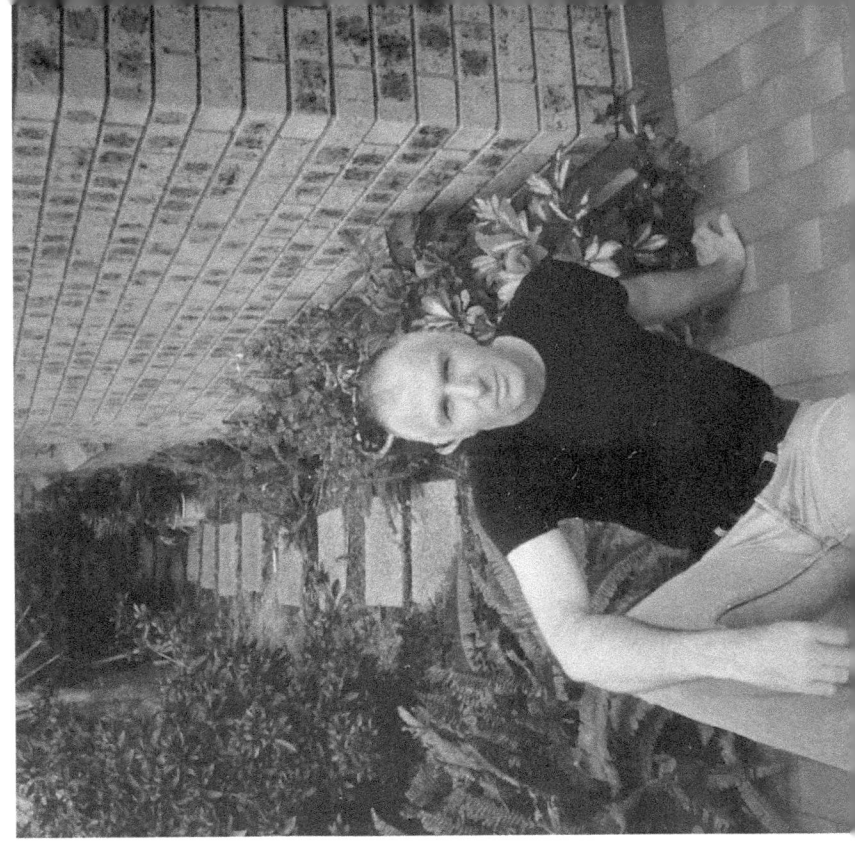

Michael Hurley,
Surry Hills, 1997.
Photographer
unknown.

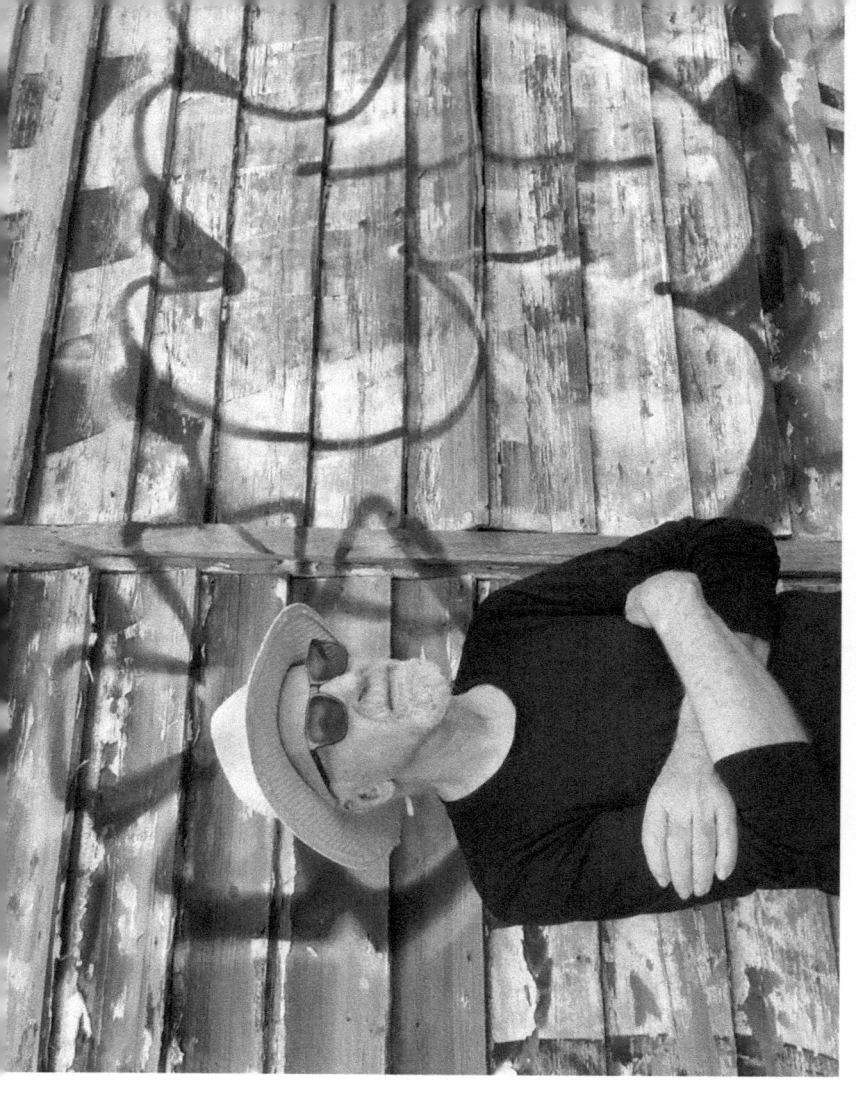

Michael Hurley,
Northcote, 2020.
Photographer:
Paul Harris

Stored away in yet another cupboard are six cobalt-blue glass goblets. A fine gold ring circles the bowl of each goblet, just below the rim. Each of the bowls is decorated with an embossed green-leafed frond, off which come six small raised white enamel flowers. Each of the flowers has a tiny yellow centre surrounded by six petals. The top three petals are tinged with blue. Ken Charnock bought them in Prague in 1991 a few short weeks before he died in St Mary's Hospital, London. Liz Jacka was in London at the time. I rang her from Australia after Ken's sister Erina told me what was happening, and Liz sat with Ken, someone she only knew slightly, until Erina and another sister Karen arrived a few days later. Erina gave the goblets to me after Karen and she returned with Ken's ashes. We planted bulbs in Killcare on the Central Coast above Sydney, made an AIDS Quilt panel and years later I wrote about these events in 'A Shopping Bag from Harrods'. All this, twenty-eight years ago. I have not forgotten. I also have Ken's art deco tea strainer that he gave me before he left on his trip. He knew, and I knew, what was going on.

I need to polish the strainer as well, so it too shines again and declares itself. It deserves to be beside the teapot.

On the same day that I polish the teapot, I read Susan Sontag's 'Writing Itself: On Roland Barthes'. It introduces her 1982 edited English collection of Barthes' translated writings. At that point, his reputation is peaking amongst Anglophone audiences, including square old monolingual putti like me. My copy comes from Jan McKemmish's library. Her partner Helen Barnes and I sorted and sifted Jan's books and papers in the years after she died. We deposited them in the State Library of Victoria. Have I read the Sontag essay previously? I cannot remember. Surely I had?

'Writing Itself' is a bravura essay, in which Sontag positions Barthes in relation to the literary history of modernism and formalism in Europe, to the dandy tradition, the writing of aesthetes and 'the repertoire of pleasure'. At one point she says,

> The aesthete's posture alternates between never being satisfied and always finding a way of being satisfied, being pleased with virtually everything.

It reads like a riff on a remark in Oscar Wilde's 1891 novel *The Picture of Dorian Gray*:

> A cigarette is the perfect type of a perfect pleasure. It is exquisite, and it leaves one unsatisfied. What more can one want?"

Unlike Oscar, or Dorian for that matter, I am not a dandy. I often dress frumpily, and am only occasionally camp in manner, though much of what I value, indeed many of my values, but not all, are influenced by camp's take on the world. As in the case of Sontag, it is possible to be too clever by half, to strain for effect, as one seeks to make one's way. Like many others I know, I live in that extended zone between the known and the unknown, between the strange and familiar, between the ordinary and the extraordinary. 'Nothing new there', as Liz Jacka might say.

Last night I saw a man in a tee shirt that said on the front, 'More Issues Than *Vogue*'. I laughed and wanted one the same.

Does camp taste presuppose in Sontag's terms 'older, high standards of discrimination?' It can. Either way, high or low, it has an eye for possibilities. It acknowledges pre-existing realities in order to mock, tease, invert, resist, theatricalise.

One might argue however that it is not just reaction, but at its best a creative response that shifts the ground on which discussion occurs. It makes space for other ways of being. At its very best, it deconstructs. It finds the pleasures that moral seriousness refuses to entertain.

I handed on my pinstriped Gaultier jacket – bought on sale at Myer in the mid 1990s, most likely in the company of Jan H. – when I couldn't button it up anymore. (Gaultier probably called it a three-button blazer. It required a degree of slenderness to be worn buttoned.) It was relatively restrained and formally stylish except for a brand insignia which I had removed. I was a contrary label queen. Perhaps it was on the breast pocket. I do not usually like visually intrusive branding, though a hint of now unfashionable Bonds or CK underwear has on occasion been known to create a frisson. I also like Gaultier's sense of theatrical extravagance, but as I age, I return often unexpectedly to the performative formalities of modernism, especially in its more geometric styles.

Earlier in the 1990s I was given an Alessi kettle I think by Jan H and Kevin. They knew I coveted it. Shiny, sleek and round with a hard polyamide scalloped handle, it was designed by Richard Sapper in 1982. It had a two-tone harmonic pitch pipe brass whistle that went off when the water boiled. Sapper is said to have based the sound on that made by boats going down the Rhine. I have the whistle still somewhere, but I burned the kettle dry so many times by leaving the whistle spout up that the kettle died. While the Alessi kettle was a great piece of mass produced high art design, an *objet de luxe*, the original stainless steel, sprung holder that you pulled to open the spout and get the water in and out overheated and burned your fingers. It was later refined. Some would say unsuccessfully.

In Amsterdam with Marshall in 2016, I walked through another gallery door, and Yves Saint Laurent's Mondrian Dress in the Rijksmuseum took my breath away. A straight vertical black line falls from the neck to the knee. A horizontal black line cuts across just above the breasts and the hem is also black. This creates a dressmaker-dummy grid on a white background with two shoulder panels between neck and breast. The upper right-hand side is yellow. The rest of the fabric is white. This style is also theatrical, but it is formal, restrained rather than wild, abstract, not representational. Fine art and fashion walk quite unexpectedly hand in hand. At this point the relevant literatures begin to talk about cubism (Picasso, Braque) and the Russian Supremacist art movement (Malevich – a self-styled 'cubo-futurist'). Ruptures in artistic convention produce new forms.

Or as Robert Hughes put it in his history of modernist art, *The Shock of the New*,

> The view from the train was not the view from the horse...the cultural conditions of seeing were starting to change.

Like John Berger's *Ways of Seeing*, eight years before, Hughes' book came from a BBC series. These are versions of a post-WWII discussion that arguably takes-off in Britain with Raymond Williams' *Culture and Society* in 1958. In Australia in the same year one might reference AA Phillips' *The Australian Tradition*, which included his 1950 essay that opposed the imposition of English tastes. He called it a 'cultural cringe'.

In the early sixties, the Victorian Racing Club added Fashions on the Field to bolster falling attendance figures, and in 1965 British model Jean

Shrimpton was invited to judge the best dress. A-line dresses, such as those in the Saint Laurent collection in the same year, including the Mondrian dress, were appearing on catwalks in the USA, Paris, London and the cover of *Vogue*. Shrimpton wore a simple white dress 10cm above her knee to Derby Day. It caused a scandal. The Melbourne establishment wanted hat, gloves and stockings. The reputed explanation for the height of the hem is prosaic. Her dressmaker, Colin Rolfe, had not been sent enough material. That version may well be apocryphal.

> The furore ... was more than just stuffiness; such freedom threatened the whole status quo. It was a pivotal moment: all the young girls wanted to be like the Shrimp, free, cool, elegant. Many young girls headed straight for the sewing box and took up their school uniform hems for the morrow.
> (Hughes, J. 2006)

Glamour and scandal walked hand in hand. These too were part of the warp and weft of everyday life. It was a year after the Beatles toured and the same year that Menzies upgraded Australia's military involvement in the Vietnam War. It was three years after the Indigenous people of Australia had been given the right to vote. Slavery and wage fraud of Aboriginal workers were rife.

Warp and weft: print and textile making provide useful metaphors for writing and for thinking about cultural politics. I take down Volume 2 of my *Shorter Oxford English Dictionary* from the bookshelves, blow off the dust (mostly these days I just google but this time I wanted the *OED*) and read, selectively:

Text: The wording of anything written or printed; the structure formed by the words in their very order.

Textile: That has been or may be woven 1656... Having markings resembling a woven surface.

Texture: The process or art of weaving

Wiki, **warp and weft:** In weaving, the weft (sometimes woof) is the thread or yarn which is drawn through, inserted over-and-under, the lengthwise warp yarns that are held in tension on a frame or loom to create cloth. Warp is the lengthwise or longitudinal thread in a roll, while weft is the transverse thread.

I gave myself the two volume *Shorter Oxford* for Christmas in 1982 or 1983. I possibly bought it in the now-gone Greville Street Bookstore in Prahran, Melbourne. Some of us were nerdy well before we could access the World Wide Web. Nerds can, however, make simple mistakes. I recall the freezing cold Friday night in a Melbourne winter in roughly the same year when I walked up from St Kilda and caught the rickety old Number 78 tram from Balaclava to the since demolished Valhalla Theatre in Victoria Street, Richmond. I was going to see what I thought was an LA street gang movie, maybe Michael Pressman's *Boulevard Nights*. It will brighten you up, I thought. I arrived slightly after the film had begun. After a few minutes, I knew whatever I was watching was not what I had come to see. It turned out to be Ridley Scott's now classic *Blade Runner*. I was buzzing the entire tram ride home.

On top of my china cabinet are a wooden Buddha and a green metal Buddha's head, both gifts from Craig, along with a fading black and white framed photo of Marlene Dietrich in a chair, another gift, this time from Murray C. I note with some surprise that there is no cigarette in her one visible hand, but then again, the right hand is hidden. The photo appears to be in a basement or cellar, but I don't think it is a shot from *The Blue Angel* (1930, Dir. Josef von Sternberg). I have carried the photo around for twenty-five years. She is wearing what appears to be a summery frock, hitched a little above her knees, and high heels. Another pair of heels lay on their sides beside her, as she sits, legs crossed, right over left, and stretched out in front. I sit back in my chair. I can hear her singing 'Falling in Love Again'. Men cluster around, singe their wings. She is not to blame.

Her face in the photo is both white lit and shadowed, almost ethereal, almost 'pure'. This is not the Dietrich of the tuxedo. It has the feel of an early studio public relations shot, the making and shaping of image in the interests of glamour, stardom and profit.

And yet when I try to find the photo online, after several searches I cannot. Nor can I explain the presence of the second pair of shoes. Was she trying out different pairs for size or comfort when the photo was taken? Is there another person just out of shot? The presence of the shoes has to be deliberate. This is not casual untidiness, or an instance of dishabille. The photo refuses to explain itself. I am longing for the shoes to be explained. I am in disarray. *Sabotage.*

The 'Blue Angel' cabaret in the film of that name was likely based to a degree on a venue called 'The Stork's Nest' (1923–1931) where Brendan Nash says, 'the songs were often filthy and suggestive and the performers more likely at the end of their career than at the start.' It was in Oranienburger Strasse in the then main Jewish area of Berlin, just north of the river Spree in Mitte. Male customers could pay to sit on the stage with the female performers and meet them later backstage where more money changed hands, and other performances probably occurred. Nash's Cabaret tour of 'Isherwood's neighbourhood' in Schöneberg is not to be missed. I have done it twice. The first time was with Marshall.

Many seem to imagine the historical Berlin cabaret scene as more like the club as depicted in *Cabaret*, the 1966 Broadway musical, later adapted by Bob Fosse in his 1972 film starring Liza Minnelli and Michael York. That's actually a somewhat more up-market club which in turn seems to me more akin to 'The Silhouette' (1926–1933), where, according to Nash, Dietrich learned in 1929 that she had been given the lead role in *The Blue Angel*: 'men and women in smoking jackets and smart suits could be seen alongside other men and women in sequined evening gowns and jewels.' On the other hand, German historian Karin Wieland in her book on Dietrich and Leni Riefenstahl refers to the Silhouette as 'a small, disreputable bar on Gaisbergstrasse' and identifies the wine bar 'Schwannecke' near the Kaiser Wilhelm church as the place where 'established theatre people and authors got together.' The person who told Dietrich of her success was Friedrich Hollaender who wrote 'Falling in Love Again' for her to sing in the film. It became one of her signature songs along with 'Lilli Marlene' and 'Where have all the Flowers Gone'. The film was Dietrich's first leading role, after eighteen roles in silent films. Wieland says 1929 was also the year that the German film industry took sound seriously. That work ethic alone suggested she had earned her spot, though it helped that von Stenberg appreciated her audition, and unlike many German actors she appears to have relished the opportunities that came with sound.

Germany came relatively late to both nationhood and democracy. It becomes a democratic republic with universal male and female suffrage in 1919, 'the Weimar Republic'. That said, Britain only gets full suffrage in 1928. The First World War and the 'peace' settlement known as the Versailles treaty had disastrous economic and political consequences in Germany over the next fifteen years. Ongoing, rapid changes of government, hyper inflation and unemployment were all rampant. Living standards deteriorated. The novelist Thomas Mann referred in a short story to the impoverished middle class as the 'the villa proletariat', but as historian Gerald Feldman suggests, it is an ironic phrase. Mann was referring to the newly straitened circumstances of the propertied rather than to poor renters of crowded rooms, between 1918–1923. Stefan Zweig began writing his autobiography *The World of Yesterday* (1942) in 1934. Wieland quotes him as writing of the 'pervert balls of Berlin, involving 'hundreds of men costumed as women, and hundreds of women as men' blaming 'a collapse of all values' for social madness. Whose values are these?

The male population had been decimated in the war, however, after the Greater Berlin Act in 1920 expanded Berlin's borders, it became the third biggest city in the world. Many single women came there seeking work. Brendan Nash estimates Berlin had a population of 85,000 lesbians. Neil Bartlett suggests that to know a city you have to search for its 'characteristic details'. Well, yes, you might say, until that city you think you know takes you yet again by surprise.

The artist Francis Bacon (1909–1992) spent time in Berlin as a young man. Daniel Farson, briefly a pub owner on London's Isle of Dogs in the East End in the early 1960s, and also a friend of Bacon's, said in his obituary of Bacon,

Homosexuality was his nature and he had the strength not to wish it otherwise. When he was 18, his father made a final attempt to 'make a man' of his son by placing him in the custody of a friend of his: a tough, no-nonsense-seeming horse trainer, but he turned out not to be what he seemed. He was a man with a taste for decadence.

They went to Berlin in about 1926 and for a while stayed in the luxurious Adlon Hotel near the Brandenburg Gate, but they clearly wandered. Bacon is reported as saying 'by way of education I found myself in the atmosphere of the Blue Angel.' By the time Bacon made the remark, it was forty years after the event.

'Atmosphere' in Bacon's remark is affective: a social mood, a collective feeling, a cultural milieu. It is the heat rising off the doing: dressing, singing, acting, drinking, drugging, dancing, flirting, fucking, paying, smelling, sweating, revelling, hurting, crying, laughing ... Bacon's remark is relatively neutral, perhaps a little ironic, but by the early sixties, that 'atmosphere' had garnered mythological status amongst those who knew it already and was about to be broadcast yet again to wider, newer audiences. The 'atmosphere of the Blue Angel' signifies an association between Weimar, cabaret and sexual freedoms of multiple kinds – a 'decadence' that values sensual and sexual expression and 'exotic' practices, especially in uncertain times, and is I suggest a little more adventurous than a good red at dinner. Robert Beachy's book *Gay Berlin. Birthplace of a modern identity* (2015) rightly locates the city's atmospheric origins well before the Weimar Republic (1919–1933) but it seems fair to say that what we are seeing in the 1920s and early 1930s is its peak. As Beachy puts it: 'there can be little doubt that Weimar Berlin was an astonishing revelation for many first-time visitors.' It is not uncommon to hear people say in their recounting of such times and events, now as well as then, 'you had to have been there.' Revelation, unveiling, begins with the gap between glove and sleeve, tee shirt and pants. You have to have been there when the glove was slowly peeled away, or the trousers came down.

Bacon appears to have stayed a while in Berlin then Paris. His mother sent him an allowance, just as Isherwood's did.

Attraction to people, places and things often comes upon me unexpectedly.

Farson's own autobiography was titled *Never a Normal Man* (1997). It is a title that manages to be simultaneously matter of fact and a touch regretful, with a *soupçon* of defiance. The book was dedicated 'To Those Who Don't Belong.' In his review, Silvester says,

> Farson is especially good at telling stories against himself. ... He asks a taxi driver to take him to an East End pub notorious for its rough trade, the Elephants' Graveyard, eliciting the inquiry, 'Excuse me, guv'ner, don't think me rude, but do you mean the boozer where young blokes go to pick up old geezers like you?'

London too has an atmosphere and a specific history. The actor John Gielgud was arrested and fined in 1953. Laurence Olivier was the subject of gossip, rumour, and eventual media exposure. In the 1950s, political sex scandals were rife: Alan Turing, the mathematician and Enigma codebreaker (1952); Edward Montagu (Lord Beaulieu) went to the police over a stolen camera and ended up in prison for a year for gross

indecency. His friends Michael Pitt-Rivers and
Peter Wildeblood were sentenced to 18 months.
The Wolfenden Committee that recommended
reform of the laws on homosexual offences and
sex work ('prostitution') sat for three years and
there was then a ten-year struggle for legalisation
of homosexual behaviour, finally achieved in 1967.
As Jeffrey Weeks put it fifty years later, 'London
was still swinging.' He goes on to say that it was
gay liberation rather than the legal changes of 1967
which made modern LGBT life what it is: 'Coming
out began to destroy the closet.' Jeanette Winterson
pointed out elsewhere on the same day that it was
fifty years of partial legalisation. Between 1967
and 2003, 'when the age of consent was equalised,
more than 30,000 men were convicted of gross
indecency.' In between came the anti-gay backlash
linked to AIDS, and Thatcher's Section 28 which
banned the promotion of homosexuality. What was
different during this period, says Weeks, was a 'new
self-confidence and public voice' that had come
with a political movement. He was right. That was
the difference Gay Liberation made.

I go back and forth in time, segueing
between the law, life, place and the mediation of
homo-cultural mainstreaming. It was the week
the governing party of the then Prime Minister
Malcolm Turnbull called for a voluntary postal vote
on Equal Marriage Rights, but one of many tortured
and tortuous manoeuvres in current versions of
Australian sex wars. These struggles over what
could and can be represented or socially approved
in public about sexual practices, legality and
associated gender matters have recurred constantly
for over a century.

Australia has not been alone in its politicised
moralism. John van Druten's 1951 play *I am a
Camera*, based on Isherwood's novel *Goodbye to*

Berlin (1939), was a Broadway hit, with the character of Sally Bowles at its centre. It ran for six months. It won the New York Drama Critics Circle Award for Best American Play, 1952. In 1955, it became a film, again called *I am a Camera*, directed by Henry Cornelius. Harper and Porter tell us that the scripting of the film ran into trouble immediately with the British Board of Film Censors (BBFC) who insisted 'that Sally Bowles be left poor and unsuccessful at film's end because of her sexual promiscuity.' It received an X certificate and flopped in cinemas. The BBFC refused a downgrade of the X classification for television viewing because Sally had an abortion. It had similar problems in the USA.

The film version of *I am a Camera* opens in a 1950s present and the lead male character, played by Laurence Olivier, tells us his name is 'Christopher Isherwood ... a novelist, set in my ways, a confirmed bachelor'. He goes to a book launch. The author is Sally Bowles. The book's title is *The Lady Goes on Hoping*. The surface of the relational dynamic is instantly heterosexualised, subject as that remark is to the coding of 'Isherwood' as a 'confirmed bachelor'. The film moves immediately to a 1931 flash back as 'Isherwood' recounts a moment when he didn't remonstrate with Nazi street thugs. 'I, I said to myself, I am a Camera'. That is, he is detached, separate, from what he witnesses. It is a confession and a regret, a filmic distancing of the character Isherwood from his past, which he remedies in his last days in Berlin. A gay couple appear momentarily in one nightclub scene in the El Dorado, itself a real cabaret until 1933. Off screen, a few scenes later, a doctor subjects the Isherwood character to a large rectal thermometer.

Cabaret's representation of queer cabaret in Berlin in the early 1930s is in part adapted from

Isherwood's first two novels *Mr Norris Changes Trains* (1935) and *Goodbye to Berlin*, as well as the play and film of *I am a Camera*. Isherwood lived in Berlin from 1929 to 1933 and wrote copious daily diary notes. The novels are set in the early 1930s during the period that Hitler and the Nazis come to power. The Weimar Republic ends in 1933. It is largely the Weimar of the twenties however that feeds the attractions evident in both Isherwood's writing and *Cabaret*. The powerful performance of Joel Grey as Master of Ceremonies in both the musical and the film reiterated the Berlin of that time as a place of decadent wickedness, mostly through the multi-sexual lives of the characters and the club scenes. The film also captures the increasing horror to come in the brown-shirted Hitler Youth member singing 'Tomorrow Belongs to me', and the persecution of Jews, homosexuals, gypsies, leftists and other minorities.

At the time of its release, *Cabaret* was amongst the liveliest, most complex, and generous representations of historical queer cultures directed to general audiences. It is arguably more revealing of wider sexual cultures than *Breakfast at Tiffany's* (1961), less demanding than *The Servant* (1963) and more mainstream (then) than *Boys in the Band* (1970). That said, some attribute to *Victim* (1961) a powerful role in advocating for legalisation of male homosexuality in the UK. It was the first British film to use the word 'homosexual'.

Cabaret crossed over, as they say, as did the original novels to an increasing degree. This was evidenced and reinforced by major awards for the film at the 1973 Academy Awards. The revivals of the musical themselves suggest a market had formed and was constantly re-forming. In the following decade, the pressure for more considered representation increased.

124

The Berlin years have been repeatedly renewed and recycled both in the name of Isherwood and in other ways. In my adult years we have seen Isherwood's memoir *Christopher and his Kind* (1976), the BBC film of the same name (2011), the film of *A Single Man* (2009), the film *Chris and Don. A love story* (2007). There are two volumes of diaries, and at least four biographies and an Isherwood encyclopaedia. The man on whom the character Mr Norris was based, Gerald Hamilton, later published an autobiography, *Mr Norris and I* (1956), and that in turn prompted biographies of him.

What we see is a living trajectory as well as a circuit of signs – not just names, but books, places, times, cultural artefacts, and excitements, forbidden and legal, yearned for, sought out and celebrated. Berlin has been and continues to be a contemporary beacon for gays and lesbians. It matters little, to many, that its glamour is often of the gritty variety, a hybrid of street, cellar, fashion, individual display, partying, uniforms, fetishes. It knows itself. That is its allure.

In this elongated circuit, 'a chain of affective images', Weimar/Berlin (then and now) signifies a place to be; good gay times, identity, Pride, sexual desire and self-revelation are linked. The continuity of temporality is, of course, interrupted by historical events, but the allure arcs, breaks and reconnects in reconstruction. As it has since with London, Sydney or any other large gay city.

Joel Grey came out at the age of 82 in 2016.

Virginia Postrel suggests that 'Glamour gives form to desire and substance to hope.' It is, she says, a way of exploring being modern. In Germany modernity largely emerged technologically – the 'modern wonders': ocean liners, aeroplanes, airships, film (first silent, then 'the talkies'), radio, domestic electricity, traffic – and in architecture

(Mies van der Rohe and the Bauhaus) and the theatre (Brecht). However this only partially explains the allure of Berlin for queers of all kinds in the twenties and early thirties, and we would also need to analyse the continuing attraction of Berlin as a city, particularly but not only, for gay men, lesbians, cross-dressers and trans people, whether gender binary or non-binary, queer or not.

There are other circuits in play alongside glamour. Often enough they involve the representation of poverty, politics, crime, and oppression. Alfred Doblin's 1929 modernist novel of lumpen proletariat life *Berlin Alexanderplatz* was filmed in 1931, made into a fourteen-part TV series by Rainer Werner Fassbinder in 1980 and informed Volker Kutscher's popular detective novels (2007–2014). The novels became the basis of the German TV series *Babylon Berlin* (2017–) that premiered in Germany and was distributed on Netflix in the USA, Canada and Australia. Arts journalist Max McGuinness recently wrote in the *Financial Times* of its murky glamour, intrigue, period authenticity and extravagant hokum. Saturated neo-noir one might say. but there was more. Set in 1929, criminality, cabaret, police corruption, murder, sex, far left political resistance and rising militarism make a heady mix. The series includes visual references to Fritz Lang's films of the 1920s and uses several tracks from Bryan Ferry's album *The Jazz Age*. Gary Dew reminds me that Ferry himself plays the band leader in some later scenes. The spirit of Bowie also hovers.

I watch series one and two of *Babylon Berlin* alone, granny rug on my legs, over several weeks. I am engrossed, savouring mesmerising scenes like that in series one, episode two where a Russian countess dressed in male character drag – leather trench coat, moustache, top hat – sings a hypnotic grinding chant while the dancing crowd mimics her movements in syncopated ecstasy until she disappears in a fiery bang. I can almost hear the director saying to the choreographer 'Don't do the cabaret scenes like *Cabaret*.' Given we know what happens in the years afterwards apocalypse looms however it is done, but this misses the point in terms of the technical bravura of the actual scene.

Amongst the reasons that Berlin stayed in public view of course were Nazism, the Second World War and the Holocaust, followed by the city's centrality in the Cold War: from the division of the city into two (East and West), the Berlin blockade, the building of the Wall, radical politics in the 1960s and 1970s, the fall of the Wall in 1989, we move to the steady emergence of Germany at the heart of the European Union and of Berlin as a city of students, immigrants, monuments and tourists.

In the Isherwood novels, we see the gay pubs where poverty-stricken working-class youths work the willing homosexual clientele for an income. It is a shared arrangement.

The 'scene' is not always glamorous, and one only knows what one knows at the time of entry into it. Naivety and wide-eyed wonder go hand in hand, at least for a while. A change of view later is not unknown. It is a source of communal identification that can also be accompanied by romantic regret. There are, however, alternatives to bitterness. Edith Piaf had no regrets for broken romances and being deceived, or so she said, and Cole Porter parodied lamentation. The 1934 Porter parody itself parlays the regret, distances it through laughter, ignores the pain – 'Miss Otis regrets she is unable to lunch today.' Piaf sang 'Miss Otis Regrets' in 1946 as have many others, before and after. Depending on how loudly it is played, the tonal force of her 1959 'Non, je ne regrette rien' however is defiant, emotionally charged, only two steps away from her version of the Marsellaise. We would do well to remember that Piaf has no regrets because a new love is growing for someone else. Many were the parties I was at in the seventies where the volume went up and drunken group singing broke out in accompaniment to both songs. We walked the line.

Sometimes I replace the photo of Marlene on top of the china cabinet with one of Dusty Springfield given to me by Rose. Other times they sit there together. The original photo of Dusty was taken by Peter Rand in 1968. In 2012 a bromide print of it was turned into a postcard as part of a National Portrait Gallery (NPG) exhibition in London of Rand's work. Rand worked for *Vogue* during the 1960s. Portraiture met celebrity, often within the frame of fashion photography. Others in the series of photos included the actor Sarah Miles, playwright Harold Pinter and entrepreneur Richard Branson. In the same year, the NPG exhibited Cecil Beaton's portraits, including a Marilyn Monroe taken in 1956 and one of Marlene from 1935. The National Portrait Gallery website says that 'the national press reported on the length of queues to get in and it had to be extended twice.'

I knew none of this when Rose gave me the postcard in 2013. What I saw was a glamorously stylised picture of Dusty Springfield with her hands to her face, looking fragile, if not fraught. I later discussed this with Rose who said that 'the hair and the clothes are sixties *femme fatale*, but the pose and her face are saying something quite different.' Her gloriously dyed, high blonde hair, carefully coiffed, bouffant, she looks out to the viewer through kohl black eyes. For me it evoked the feeling of her mid-sixties singing, riffing as it does on soul and Motown. Springfield herself spoke of the photo as representing 'the other me'. Biographer, Rebecca Jennings, tells us Dusty came from a troubled home, was a Roman Catholic, a lesbian and for much of her career feared exposure. Stardom gave room to pass, however ambiguously, as straight. I first sang along to her music with her solo hit 'I only wanna be with you' in 1963. I doubt Rose knew that.

Popular music expert Tony Mitchell at UTS pointed out in 2001 that this was the first song ever to be featured on the BBC TV music program Top of the Pops, on New Years' Day in 1964.

Six to eight years after 'I only wanna be with you' was released I read James Baldwin's bestselling novel *Another Country* (1962) where he wrote about race and sex, or as Professor of Literature Claudia Pierpont put it in the *New Yorker*, 'black rage, interracial sex, homosexuality, white guilt, urban malaise'. Maybe it was 1972, the same year I read Dennis Altman's *Homosexual. Oppression and Liberation*. That I do remember. During the 1960s, as Dusty Springfield's career developed, 'Baldwin', says Altman, 'perceived the extent to which oppression was ingrained in the very marrow of American society.' Why, asked Baldwin, would one want to be integrated into that? I thought it a good question then, and by and large still do.

Dusty's early musical roots were in Afro-American jazz and Jelly Ray Morton's blues, Billie Holiday, Ella Fitzgerald, Dionne Warwick, with her own crossovers into pop with a country edge. Her 1964 first solo album had seven covers of songs previously performed by African American singers. That same year, 1964, she was forced to leave South Africa for refusing to sing to segregated audiences. She had included this refusal in her contract. In the following year, she was instrumental in bringing the Supremes, Smokey Robinson and the

Miracles, Martha Reeves and the Vandellas, Stevie Wonder, and the Temptations to prime-time British television on *Ready, Steady, Go*.

This was not the world of *Coronation Street* which first aired five nights a week in 1960 and is still being produced. Black people have lived in Britain for centuries. The first ongoing black character in *Coronation Street* did not appear until the early 1980s. An Asian (Indian) family appeared in 1999, and an openly gay male character appeared in 2001. Lesbian characters began to appear after 2009. The price of strong characters, good scripting and acting, compounded by a regional setting, was massive cultural lag. It was first aired in Australia in 1963 and by 1966 is said to have been more popular here than it was in the UK.

Karen Bartlett quotes one of Dusty's girlfriends, Norma Tanega, as saying "she wanted to be straight and she wanted to be a good Catholic and she wanted to be black'. Under the pressure of her own demons, alcohol and social hostility to homosexuality, she often sought treatment and over time her career faltered badly. By 1985 she was miming to her own hits in West Hollywood gay bars, loved by her audiences, and being paid $500 a night, even so... Two years later she did a duet with the Pet Shop Boys who were also involved with her next two singles as she relaunched her career.

As mentioned earlier, there is a difference between taking on an identity as one's own – I'm lesbian /gay /bi/straight /trans – and identification. Halperin also points out that identification is not a random process. There are points of identification. At least initially, Dusty identified musically. She adopted specific musical genres and that involved on her part an engagement with the social and cultural milieu from which they came. She formed a relationship with the sounds and those who made them. She was not alone in this of course. Rock and Roll preceded her. It had crossed over from black culture to white teenagers *en masse* by the mid 1950s with Bill Haley's 'Rock around the Clock' and Chuck Berry's 'Maybellene'.

While some saw Elvis as ripping off black music and making a killing from it, for Dusty Springfield identification, however awkwardly expressed, became a form of political solidarity. Pop critic Jack Hamilton reports a 1964 *Melody Maker* interview in which Dusty says,

> I have a real bond with the music of the coloured artists in the States. I feel more at ease with them than I do with many white people...I wish I'd been born coloured. When it comes to singing and feeling, I just want to be one of them and not me. Then again, I see how some of them are treated and I thank God I'm white.

Ok, it is a bit messy and naive, but it is also a direct, honest statement of support. In combination with her actions, I see it as honourable. She did it when others did not, did it first and after she did others criticised her for doing so. At the airport as she was climbing the steps to her BOAC jet home from South Africa 'black ground staff, in a spontaneous act of solidarity formed a guard of honour.'

Dusty died aged fifty-nine in 1999. She had a Catholic funeral.

Mitchell says that shortly after Springfield's death, Elton John 'memorialised her as the greatest white singer there has ever been.' Mitchell uses Barthes' notion of 'the grain of the voice' to analyse the respect Springfield had for the sounds she was making, their sexuality, their sentimentality and sensuality, to give in Barthes' terms 'the impossible account of an individual thrill' and a process which 'sways us to *jouissance*.'

> The power of Springfield's voice, with all its affective associations, to evoke emotions, memories, and feelings is her most memorable and lasting feature ...

'Jouissance' as the word is used by Roland Barthes is a form of bliss. It may have a sense of the ecstatic or the orgasmic that comes as a reader disrupts the text in the process of reading. It can also induce a sense of loss and discomfort as the text disrupts the reader's assumptions.

Mitchell saw Elton John's use of 'white' as 'an assertion of an essentialised postcolonial Britishness'. That is, Britain still thought of itself as white. He quotes bell hooks: 'To ignore white ethnicity is to redouble its hegemony by naturalising it.' Richard Dyer took on this challenge of denaturalising in his book *White* (1997):

> whites must be seen to be white, yet whiteness as race resides in invisible properties and whiteness as power is maintained by being unseen.

In the Australian context, Paul Keating, in 1996 put it this way when he spoke of Pauline Hanson and the racial politics of One Nation: 'The myth of the monoculture. The lie that we can retreat to it.'

I have another Dietrich photo, also a postcard, this time one Graham Willett sent me from Germany. It is a waist-up shot from *Morocco* (1930): tuxedo jacket, top hat, high-collared white shirt, white bow tie and a very white cigarette sticking out of her lip sticked mouth. One side of her face is lit, the other in shadow. The total effect is one of piss elegance, or as others might say, 'smart sophistication'. The photographer Eugene Robert Richee headed Paramount's portrait studio. His photo shoots were often overseen by Josef von Sternberg who directed Dietrich in seven films. American film critic David Kehr said of the characters played by Dietrich that they

> function both as objects of desire (her face drinks in light like a Brancusi sculpture) and agents of desire, in the grip of consuming, concentrated loves that frequently demand pain or martyrdom.

If one only saw the lighting, (partially white-lit faces accentuated by shadow), many of Richee's photos of Dietrich and other actors might seem similar. They are, but the detail of the compositions, the clothes, and the specifics of the actors involved, what is done with their hair, their faces, makeup, what is done with the hands, the angle of the body etc, need to be addressed. It is cinematic stylisation – Hollywood-style glamour.

These images of Marlene and Dusty are a public form of carefully modulated visual rhetoric. They are highly productive in the sense that as they circulate as images in relation to both sound and celebrity they generate and support professionally managed careers and stardom. These matters are often pitched against a lack of sincerity and authenticity, but they are no less 'real', no less 'true' than warts and all personalised accounts of the private person. Fans freewheel in fandom. They are absorbed.

Graham wrote on the back of the postcard:

> Some postcards cry out to be bought & tell you who to buy them for. Cute boys all over (the city, not me). Work in the morning, tourist

133

in the arvo, friends in the evening. There are worse ways to spend your day.

He knows me well. We were both in Berlin in 2009, my first visit since 1974, and again in 2015, when we went and visited Marlene's grave together. The gravestone reads *Hier steh ich an den Marken meiner Tage*. One translation of this is 'Here I stand at the milestone of my days.', Marlene 1901–1992.

A literal translation I found said 'marks' of her life rather than 'milestone'. The marks are legendary: a string of female and male lovers, a husband, the wearing of trousers, cabaret, singing sultrily, acting, parenting, anti-Nazi concerts during the war, gender bending and glamour. According to the *Guardian*'s *Observer* archive she said in 1960,

> I dress for the image. Not for myself, not for the public, not for fashion, not for men. ...If I dressed for myself I wouldn't bother at all. Clothes bore me. I'd wear jeans. I adore jeans. I get them in a public store – men's, of course; I can't wear women's trousers. But I dress for the profession.

Graham's use of 'boys' (young men) is straight from the pages of Isherwood. If not from the first two novels then the later memoir *Christopher and His Kind* (1976) where he speaks of his younger self in the third person: 'To Christopher, Berlin meant boys'. 'Boys' in Sydney in the 1980s meant any gay male under 40, if not just any gay man of whatever age. After 40 though, one's presence in some venues brought mutterings of 'it must be pension day.'

Marlene knew the 1920s cabaret scene in Schöneberg, Berlin. She was born there. Her father was a cop. They lived above the local police station, before moving on several times.

In 1960 I was eleven. I knew nothing of any of this. I lived with my family in army domestic quarters in regional northern Victoria. Nearby, across a paddock, and over the creek, were junk yards full of broken-down tanks and army ducks that in hindsight matched the vehicles in the post-war Movietone newsreels and the war films still showing in the army picture theatre. By 1962 or so whoever ordered the films had programmed Robert Weine's *The Cabinet of Dr Caligari* (1920) on a Tuesday night. I saw the 'shorts' (trailer) on the previous Saturday and asked my parents if I could go. They like me were a bit mystified by my choice, but the optic spinning wheels of graphic insanity had caught my attention. Critics refer to it as German Expressionism at its filmic best. I suspect, however, given the usual film fare at the theatre, the programmer thought they were getting the largely unrelated but just released *The Cabinet of Caligari*, directed by Roger Kay. Its title rides on the reputation of its German predecessor, along with a central plot twist but not much else. Perhaps on the following Saturday, cultural lag in a regional army picture theatre being what it was, we watched William Wyler's 1959 *Ben Hur*. We loved a wide screen blockbuster. Jews resist imperial Rome and everyone, almost two millennia later, goes off to the matinee crucifixion.

I was living in a strange interim space somewhere between the aftermath of WWII and the Beatles World Tour in 1964, caught between army shoes, regional social conservatism and stove pipe 'pegged' pants.

Before catching up with Graham in Berlin in 2015, I meet up in Hamburg with Wiebke Störtenbecker, an old friend from Sydney

University, and her partner Hinrich. Wiebke and I met there once before in the early seventies at her aunt's where I developed a taste for a brown rice and onions fry-up for breakfast. We caught a bus through then East Germany to Berlin for a few days before hitchhiking down to Cologne, then making our way to Koblenz, Heidelberg and Freiburg and on to Spain. I had not seen Wiebke since the early nineties and this time we go to a one-woman performance that recreates the program of a concert Dietrich did in Hamburg in 1960. There are perhaps fifty in the audience half of whom might have been twenty to thirty years old at the time of Dietrich's original performance. It is a Sunday afternoon and they are well dressed. The singer, herself well into middle age, performed the songs in the order Dietrich had sung them, and spoke of Dietrich's life and performances between the numbers. Wiebke translated so I understood bits, topic headings. The singer wore the tuxedo in the second half. I found it deeply satisfying.

In 1932, it was the trousers that most bothered people and the contexts in which she wore them. Fashion commentator Harriet Fisher wrote that Marlene was the first Hollywood actress to wear trousers in public though women in Paris had been wearing them for years, and Marlene had also worn them previously in Josef von Sternberg's *Morocco*. A tuxedo is not intrinsically sexed. It is simply a textile tailored to a pattern. In that sense the 'style' is neutral, however Dietrich was a woman who wore men's clothes. The 'pattern' was cultured, socialised, gendered. Yet she was disguising nothing. She challenged dress codes for women. This is not Tilda Swinton playing a nobleman magically becoming a woman in Sally Potter's film adaptation (1992) of Virginia Woolf's *Orlando* (1928) where the male character she plays is an ephebe, smooth skinned, fluid, without an underlined masculinity. That is the point of course. Genders can also be liminal in appearance, fluidly practised, 'cut' this way not that.

Liminal: a space in between, a threshold between what has been and what might be.

I need to reread Joan Nestle's 1992 edited collection *The Persistent Desire. A Femme-Butch Reader*. There's more to these matters than gender alone. Jeanne Cordova: 'When I comb my hair back and strut out my front door, being butch is my hallelujah.' Joan notes too how the streets were often hostile: 'bulldyke' was an epithet. One needs to remember how binary gender was and often still is vigorously socially policed.

Dietrich enunciated and managed her attitude to male clothes differently at different times – practicality, glamour, necessity. It is also clear that mischievousness, disdain and self-determination were in play. It was not a matter of deception.

Her daughter Maria Riva put it this way in the documentary *No Angel*: 'She was a magnificent actress and very alive, much better in real life than she was on the screen.'

Performativity, the staging of one's life, and what others think of it. In Riva's case, not just any 'other', but a mother spoken of ambiguously in relation to the framing of image: Dietrich.

Dietrich was glamorous but rarely conventionally so, and women in tuxedos, with or without a monocle, were often seen as scandalous. As Rebecca Kennison said in the *Journal of Lesbian Studies*, butch and femme muck up dichotomies too rigidly bound to gender and sexual identity. Play, pleasure and social defiance do just that.

In 1966 Saint Laurent designed 'Le Smoking' – a tuxedo-style suit for women – which was worn by amongst others Catherine Deneuve, Lauren Bacall and Bianca Jagger. However, the suit's fame came with a Helmut Newton black and white photoshoot published in the French edition of *Vogue* in 1975. It is shot at night in the Rue Aubriot in the Marais. The lighting is naturalistic. The model is Vibeke Knudsen-Bergeron. Her hair is short and slicked, her stance rakish. She leans slightly back, one knee bent, a cigarette in her right hand, the left hand in her pocket. She looks down, musing, but emanates composed confidence. She is neither demure nor discreet. Years later, in the *New York Times*, Christopher Benfey wrote of the image,

> The woman in the photograph evokes a familiar figure from 19th-century French art, the cold-eyed (and always male) dandy who, in Baudelaire's famous formulation, has "no profession other than elegance".

Dietrich demanded in her actions that what was possible for women be rethought. She did it with style and died in Paris aged ninety. I take note, but rents are high.

III

IV

As I look at the Dietrich photo on the top of the china cabinet again, the lighting this time reminds me of Greta Garbo who starred in the 1933 American produced film, *Queen Christina*, directed by Rouben Mamoulian. Decades ago, Leigh alerted me to how at the end of the film she stands in the bow of a boat looking forward. We went to see it. I was mesmerised. It is a sublime moment.

Earlier in the film, Christina is admonished by her Chancellor, 'But your Majesty, you cannot die an old maid.' Her defiant reply is, 'I have no intention to, Chancellor. I shall die a *bachelor*.' Journalist Alex Smith in 2005 quoted a letter from Garbo to one of her suitors: 'I will probably remain a bachelor all my life. Wife is such an uggly [sic] word.' Barthes wrote in *Mythologies* (1957) that the image of her face was all, 'a kind of absolute state of the flesh, which could be neither reached nor renounced.' At that moment audiences, he suggests, are lost in an image of the flesh, damned in the process by a loss of self. Lost, I wonder, no longer to be found, or distracted from the self? In that sublime moment of delight, awe, reverence, surely one is found outside of the self. It is sacrilege of course to claim that one is found when looking at an image, a graven one at that: the moving image as engraved moment, memory of it a receptacle of what is lost. Protestantism comes flying through: 'Once I was lost, but now I'm found.' Metaphors are powerful: 'was blind, but now I see.' Yes, mythology, but so much more to be felt, thought, and said as well. I am bothered that Barthes seemed bothered by ecstasy. I have to remind myself he wrote this in the early 1950s. Twenty years later he was writing of jouissance. Ecstatic secularism has its day, but the urge to confess comes upon me: 'Amazing Grace' gets me every time.

In celebrity media terms, these states of the flesh are reduced to Garbo, 'The Divine' versus Dietrich, 'The Empress of Desire.' I see no reason why one can't aspire simultaneously to luminosity and desirability.

Julie Bishop and I watched the whirling dervishes in Istanbul. The dervishes went for over an hour, starting slow, building rhythms, picking up speed, twirling, peaking, slowing, re-forming, building up the rhythm again and again. We were entranced, mesmerised: hypnotic physical meditation. Not dancing, whirling, seeing the face of god on all sides.

I have two small spice bowls that Julie gave me as a gift on that trip, one blue, one green, with black rims. In the centre of each is a dervish in classic swirling white robes and in this case, red pointed hats. In the green bowl the arms are out stretched. In the blue they are bent at the elbows at shoulder height, hands clasped. They take me back every time I use them. Mostly I do so at Christmas which has its own little ironies.

Is all this a distracted version of what happens when I am 'in' my cups, exploring their physicality, their design, their history, their giftedness? In a way, yes. I see again, bring back into view, the value and importance of friendship in my life, of more than passing contentment, of what it has made possible, what we give to each other, what we share and the productivity of putting ego out of the way in everyday relations. They signal a continuity that momentarily pushes the seriality of meeting in person to the side, yet both aspects are there, sometimes long lasting, sometimes transient; friendships structure flows of contact, sometimes frequent, sometimes not. They also come and go. There are other ways of speaking friendship than through gifts. The cups, saucers, plates however persist whatever stories I attach to them. I have invested sufficiently in them in this writing not to want to think of them broken.

It disturbs some that Barthes never 'came out' in the public sphere. That does not mean he was not out to those he knew, and it seems to me very likely his sexuality was a relatively 'open secret'. He was 'outed' officially when his literary executor published *Incidents* (1987. Tr. 1992) which included two pieces Barthes had written about cruising for sex with men. His first biographer, Louis-Jean Calvet, notes Bathes never campaigned about it. On the surface, it is a factual note, but there are other surfaces, a worrying at it. Calvet puts it down to Barthes not wanting to upset his mother. Campaigning is one thing, I have done my share, and sometimes still do, the everyday living of outness another. It is not as though Barthes was silent on all political matters. He was not a militant but was critical of France's war against Algerian independence in the mid to later 1950s and was generally seen as a non-Stalinist leftist.

I am not a scholar of Barthes, Dietrich or Garbo. I just like them. Reviewing Calvet's biography of Barthes, Ben Rogers wrote of Barthes that,

> He combined a Protestant passion for order and routine with nights in Tunisian brothels and Parisian gay bars. He was a radical critic of the fashion system who liked classic English clothes, a Marxist who recoiled from '68, a champion of hedonism who never publicly proclaimed his homosexuality.

I wonder whether the reviewer perceived Tunisian brothels and Parisian gay bars as dis-orderly and rowdy simply because of what he imagined they were. Most bars of whatever kind get somewhat raucous after a certain time of night. Contrary to the reviewer, brothels are ordered spaces that in both senses 'contain' rowdiness.

Barthes published his book *Roland Barthes* in 1975. It was translated into English in 1977. Amongst other things it addresses the nature of autobiography. He uses himself to explore what it means to be a biographical object. He is the text. In one section of the book Barthes lists his likes and dislikes. His dislikes include 'the politico-sexual, scenes, initiatives, fidelity, spontaneity, evenings with people I don't know etc'. He must have found bar life largely intolerable. In the next paragraph, he sees the items on the list as producing an 'anarchic foam of tastes and distastes, a kind of listless blur' out of which comes 'the figure of bodily enigma, requiring complicity or irritation.' He mixes figurative rhetoric and associated personal discomforts:

> Here begins the intimidation of the body, which obliges others to endure me *liberally*, to remain silent and polite confronted by pleasures or rejections which they do not share.

His interest biographically is in the relation between the presence of the body (his in this case) and social interaction. He is intimidated by reactions to his bodily presence which seems to require a liberal endurance on the part of others. It is an interesting change of emphasis from, if not refusal of, the more familiar phrase, 'liberal tolerance.' A tolerance that some of us went past with gusto when after reading Altman's *Homosexual* we demanded acceptance. I am not so sure now in the current rush to the social mainstream that these terms can be so easily opposed, but that is not the point here. Barthes sidestepped such political thinking. On his account he is someone to be socially endured. Speaking of his pleasures socially elicits silence. He could have been speaking of others' dislike of tea and madeleines but the surrounding context suggests otherwise. (He does point out that Proust was alive in his childhood.) Barthes resents that it is he in one part of his social world who has to be liberal in response by establishing a formal distance from the self, and a complicity with polite forms of social interaction. He's a cranky old buggar really, and smart as he is, fustian. He's not alone in that. What emerges for him is a tiresome detached formal civility forged out of social necessity not the freely shared mutuality that comes with intimates. He positions himself as separate. His tastes, not those of an anarchic sociality, are the standard by which all else is judged. There is not much give here, little room for pleasure either way, except perhaps in the satisfaction that may have come from the writing in of himself as he explores the nature of biography. Control issues abound. He is neither wistful for nor demanding of social acceptance. I feel a sneaking admiration, an unexpected affinity. Riotous behaviour in my wardrobe mirror anyone?

An ageing gay male cross-dressing acquaintance who entertains gentlemen callers once told me much if not all depends on the lighting. Illusion requires it.

Being in or out is like Melbourne weather – 'four seasons every day'. Family and employment often add complication and caution and people learn to weave their way through these adroitly in the interests of their sanity, equanimity and relative safety. As my Canadian friend Terry Goldie put it in his *queersexlife* (2008), one can be out and not out simultaneously. He speaks as a sometime crossdresser, a father, a gay man, a lover of women. Being out becomes a contextual act, a tactical practice, a sometimes thought, sometimes unthinking matter of how one behaves on the tram, the bus, a train, in the classroom, at weddings, at funerals or over dinner. Add serious grief to the mix and the complications multiply. Much depends on who is whispering what to whom. Barthes was out to some friends and not to others.

In the early 1970s a priestly acquaintance of a certain style referred to me as 'Michael "I'm a homosexual" Hurley.' He didn't like being pressured to come out. My mouthy militancy had become a thorn in his side.

I recently bought and potted a vibrantly coloured magenta verbena. It shouts its presence.

In Dino Hodge's biography of the former South Australian Premier, Don Dunstan, he discusses Dunstan, using a distinction between personal coming out ('I am') and publicly identifying with community.

> Dunstan had chosen to 'come out' in a characteristically idiosyncratic manner: by making an act of personal identification with community without making a statement of individual identity.

That coming out moment was in the late 1990s at an event around the first Feast Festival celebrating gay and lesbian communities in Adelaide. I spoke or read at Feast two or three times but cannot remember whether I was at this one. Despite Dunstan's personal life having attracted media, community, police and political attention over the previous forty years, choosing to identify in this way was not surprising. He had a wide civil liberties and reform agenda that included reining in some police powers.

He did not want to compromise that. It is likely he had had a police Special Branch file from the early 1960s, if not the early 1950s when he campaigned against banning the Communist Party. He was harassed by police manoeuvring and the media for much of the seventies, and it is not too extreme to say he was hounded out of office as Premier.

As Dino recounts, Dunstan later resigned as the Chairman of the Victorian Tourism Commission in 1986. This followed a manufactured political scandal around pictures taken with audience members at the launch of Garry Wotherspoon's edited collection of gay men's life stories, *Being Different*, at Sydney Town Hall. I was there with Leigh, who had a chapter in the book – 'Piss Elegant from Shit Creek.' He signed my copy. I still have it. Craig, then a Sydney city alderman, had organised the venue. Nicholas Rothwell reported in the *Australian* that 'the star attraction Monsignor Porcamadonna' (sic) (Fabian lo Schiavo) 'appeared from the colonnades where he had been adjusting his regalia':

> Clad in resplendent scarlet robes, with a bright cross of stage rubies and diamonds flashing on his habit, he gave the new book his formal blessing and imprimatur.

The photograph accompanying the news report included 'Mr Toby Zoates', Don Dunstan, 'Mr Garry Wotherspoon', Fabian and 'Mr Leigh Raymond.' A media storm erupted in Victoria accompanied by a homophobic attack from the opposition Liberal Party, led by Jeff Kennett. Kennett's campaign went national and affected the Cain Labor government in Victoria. Dunstan resigned. He was a Labor stalwart. Craig was censured by Sydney City Council for organising such a 'disgraceful event'.

The year before, in 1985, Craig had initiated the first AIDS Candlelight Vigil. He tells me it was coordinated by him and Brian McGahen, also then an alderman on Sydney City Council, and organised at a meeting of their supporters. Brian died in 1990.

Barthes was not a street activist. His political interventions were written. In 1960, he met Phillipe Sollers who was twenty years younger. Over time they became friends. Calvet wrote: 'The former [Barthes] was discreetly homosexual, while the latter flaunted his homosexuality. Barthes was suspicious of any form of exhibitionism'.

Dunstan was famed for wearing pink shorts in parliament. Dino argues that an over focus on this event disguises the complexity of what was occurring under Dunstan's leadership of the state. I agree, but it is also the case it was a gloriously mischievous and defiant moment that gave and still gives pleasure to many. I do not know whether Dunstan ever regretted his action or commented on the costs of his audacity.

Barthes' support for Algerian independence leads me to re-watch Fred Zimmerman's *The Day of the Jackal* (1973) which dramatizes the attempts to kill President de Gaulle in the early 1960s for granting Algeria independence after years of war. 'We are not terrorists', say the secret right-wing army organisation the OAS 'we are patriots.' Whatever. The Citroens and Peugeots are a joy. At another time, I will re-watch Gillo Pontecorvo's *The Battle of Algiers* (1966). Given the relative cinematic tautness of *The Day of the Jackal*, I suspect Zimmerman may have also.

I go to my bookshelves once more and pull out Renaud Camus' *Tricks* (1979). It is a chronicle of Camus' sexual encounters with men in France and other countries. I have the 1981 version published by St Martin's Press, New York. The back cover has endorsements by Allen Ginsberg, Dennis Altman and Seymour Kleinberg. Each at that time was known internationally for writing and publishing on gay matters. Barthes wrote the Preface which he was wont to do when asked to by friends or thought it useful to do so. He was about 64 by then. One assumes he wrote it in the year after his mother died. There is an unruliness in personal grief, but death also frees.

In the Preface Barthes says amongst other things that

> Homosexuality shocks less, but continues to be interesting; it is still at that stage of excitation where it provokes what might be called feats of discourse ...

He says this in a Preface to what we might call a homosexual book. He is there and not there. He attaches his name and reputation to the book but refuses to endorse speaking out in the name of homosexuality. The events described in the narratives, the encounters, he says 'speak homosexuality, but never speak about it ... They are surfaces without shadows, without ulterior motives.' There is more than one way to be saved it seems.

The American literary professor D.A. Miller said in reference to Barthes, that what we see is a phobic refusal to be named as gay. Edmund White wrote of Proust that while he was 'eager to make love to other young men, he was equally determined to avoid the label "homosexual".' Many live in that social space still, just as many others of us to varying degrees act in spite of fear or refuse to act because of it. 'Discretion required' is not uncommon in individual profiles on gay phone apps. Sometimes discretion is a matter of cultural negotiation and of what one is and is not prepared to sacrifice in relation to family, employment, friends. I have learned to respect it more than I once did. These are individual decisions, but ongoing public resistance to homophobia is politically necessary. Even after two decades of celebrity coming out, ubiquitous in western countries, horrific murders and assaults still occur here and even more so elsewhere. Legal and social advances require constant defence, even in the west. Many, especially but not only, internationally, still need room for careful manoeuvre: Russia, Chechnya, Nigeria ...the how of support is all important. As Altman and Symons put it in *Queer Wars* (2016),

> Writing from the privileged safety of a liberal-democratic state, we are aware that advocates of international change must be cautious in urging action upon others...western advocacy should focus on building an international consensus protecting sexual minorities from violence and persecution

There is often enough a precariousness in ordinary social interactions requiring a learned mix of thoughtfulness, attention, kindness and a degree of delicacy in manoeuvre. Brusqueness and directness are often not the best way to go. Hence 'liberal endurance', an itchy tolerance accompanied by discomforted grumpiness. I find it hard to imagine Barthes laughing uproariously, as distinct from the possibility of being spellbound by him (and perhaps made impatient).

Social and sexual interactions, more generally, are often governed by pressing or urgent political necessities. I think of movements for civil rights, against Aboriginal deaths in custody, health emergencies such as access to AIDS treatments and HIV prevention, legalising abortion, sex education and safe schools. It is true there are often personal costs to speaking out. That is not an argument against doing so. It is both a tactical and strategic issue.

Some days, I find I also empathise with Greta Garbo as the neurasthenic Russian ballerina in *Grand Hotel* (1932): 'I want to be alone.' Barthes was forty-one when *Mythologies* was published. I was eight. When I was about fourteen, I found a thick paperback copy of Simone de Beauvoir's *The Second Sex* (1949), which was first published in English in 1953. It was toward the back of the highest shelf in the hall cupboard. Put there, I have no doubt, to be out of sight of prying eyes, though by which of my parents I don't know. Memory says it had a somewhat glossy cover of a semi-naked woman and the word 'sex' in the title leapt from the page. It looked like a very rude book. Given that my father usually read Larry and Stretch westerns set in Texas though written in Australia – I read them after him – its presence was quite unexpected. It is not impossible my mother had bought it. I think that is unlikely, but then again, she did take me by surprise one day in the mid-sixties when she said to him in a quarrel, 'Who do you think you are, Bluebeard?' Either way, we were after all in an army camp outside of Wodonga, it was hardly Paris – Paris, Texas more like, without Ry Cooder's soundtrack. Think weekly parades which required the preparation of belts, boots and brass buckles. Much polishing and ironing was involved. Mostly it happened the night before but was sometimes redone the morning of the parade. Tension abounded. Belts had multiple uses. Around that time, I walked through Wodonga on a hot Sunday afternoon in suede boots, flared jeans and a brown shirt with white polka dots. There was almost no one to be seen (pop. c.4000). I felt very out of place.

I was. By then our first television set had arrived. I was in Carnaby Street.

I read *The Second Sex* surreptitiously, with interest. I doubt I made head nor tail of it. I read it again I think in 1971. It was still difficult reading, but I was also reading Germaine Greer's *The Female Eunuch* (1970), and Betty Friedan. It was no longer the fifties, yet I was also still enjoying that gloriously solitary pleasure: reading. By then, however, reading was inextricably linked to talking constantly with others about ideas, gender and politics. It was probably 1971 in a shared house in Redfern that I also read de Beauvoir's *The Mandarins* (1954), for a long time one of my favourite novels. I cannot remember now the paragraph in it that gave me great solace and which I quoted interminably, but I note the title. Mandarins are people with interest and influence in literary, social and political circles.

Elegance, for dandies, says Sontag, 'equals the largest amount of refusal.' I quote that to refer to Dietrich and Garbo, pre-isolation, not to me. I am about to write that I am not sure what it means other than being a dressy fuck you, and how in many ways I like that, but I think also about bodily ageing and the anxieties of attraction, the fear of not being wanted, and of wanting not to be ruled by fear. A friend reminds me to be grateful for gerontophilia. I am. Sometimes layers can be kept on.

In the UK, France and the USA, Black dandyism is alive and dressing. It has also had a strong presence in the Democratic Republic of the Congo and the Republic of Congo through the 'Society of Ambiance-Makers and Elegant People'. Ekow Eshun, a former editor of the British men's fashion magazine *Arena* and former Director of the Institute of Contemporary Art in London, writes:

Dandyism, defined as a man "unduly concerned with looking stylish and fashionable", might seem like trivial concerns in the era of the Black Lives Matter campaign. But as the case of Trayvon Martin, shot by George Zimmerman for looking "suspicious" in a hoodie, attests to the fact that how you dress can sometimes be the difference between life and death.

Baudelaire had a somewhat different take:

Dandyism is the last flicker of heroism in decadent ages… Dandyism is a setting sun; like the declining star, it is magnificent, without heat and full of melancholy.

Contexts change. Much depends on your social situation. This time I think of IT millennials and populist rich political mavericks, of untrammelled profiteering, and the possibility of new forms of aristocracy coming to power.

I digress too readily. Let us momentarily bring the teapot back into view. My pleasure with this object is not only with its physical materiality and design. It is also with the way it acts for me as a producer of memory. I know myself through it. I write myself with it, and in that process of writing – tiring and tireless – renew my own liveliness. I drink tea and muse and talk and write. Tea is, after all, a refreshing beverage, restorative, and in its own gentle way a stimulant. The pot, separate from, and alongside, the other objects in the china cabinet, produces more general memories of social interactions, events, friends, strangers, acquaintances, institutions, rallies, meetings, ideas, books, of some of what it is that has constituted my life.

155

Several weeks after I write that last paragraph, Lynne Segal draws my attention to Matt Cook's *Queer Domesticities*. In a section he partly sub-titles 'the queer comfort of things', Cook tells a story of how a photograph once owned by Wilde has been passed from one friend to another – from Wilde to Robbie Ross, to Duncan Grant, to Simon Watney until it reached Neil Bartlett. 'The tiny erotic image of a young man is now imbued with its journey and with each of its owners.' Each of those beneficiaries is a figure in internationally relayed stories of British male homosexuality.

I fancy myself momentarily – oh the vanity – as a bricoleur, a creator who uses materials at hand to make something, but a textual montage made out of a series of quotes, narrative devices, timings, placement, is more than bricolage. What is at hand is not totally random, though access to the web perhaps makes that more possible. These are not found objects in my cabinet. They are selected by the givers, then placed by me for cabinet display and then again selected for mention. I riff on them, bring trainings into play, draw on cultural capital, discover the embedded nature of my personal preferences and perhaps pretensions. Even so, as Stuart Hall says in the front matter of *Familiar Stranger*,

> One simply cannot and will never be able to fully recuperate one's own processes of thought or creativity self-reflexively ... I cannot become identical with myself.

Writing life has its challenges. Writing is always about selection including when describing the making of a life – emphases, themes, narrative devices and structures. Naming names in the process, as I have done here is invidious. Not only have other friends given me gifts, their friendship alone is a gift. Not being named does not mean you do not count. You are remembered.

'Sometimes we do things we don't quite understand.' It is a line from Kay Pollack's Swedish film, *As it is in Heaven* (2004). Writing is often like that for me. I find out where I am going with it in the doing. Like jazz, my less academic writing is often improvised and formally loose. It can segue abruptly. It quotes others and over time sometimes requotes itself – phrases, through lines, incidents, anecdotes. There is repetition, recurrence. It weaves its way through, calling, invoking, responding. I am talking in hindsight of course, and as I say it is less apparent in my more academic work which was often governed by the tight generic conventions and word length restrictions required by refereed journals.

As is the case for many writers, much of my writing has been occasional, produced by circumstance (obituaries), or by invitation (book launches, birthday celebrations, literary events, book reviews). Other times, it was produced for oral presentation at conferences, seminars and workshops, for publication as journal articles or book chapters or research monographs. It has only sometimes been written in overtly literary forms: the book, the short story, the poem, the essay, 'real' books, 'proper' writing.

I skate across surfaces, twirling.

Lesley Podesta published one of my first bits of fiction in 1980 when she was co-editor of a Melbourne University student orientation publication. I wrote then under the pseudonym Roger Casement. Casement was a British diplomat and Irish republican executed for treason in 1916. Appeals for clemency were undercut by the release of his diaries that detailed some of his homosexual encounters. I went on to publish occasional stories,

book reviews and articles in *Gay Community News*,
Outrage, *Campaign*, the *Sydney Star Observer*
the *National AIDS Bulletin* and *HIV Australia*.
To my surprise, Lesley was also at an Australian
Sociological Association conference in Perth in
1991, where I had been invited to present on HIV/
AIDS. I found out later that my colleague Jeannie
Martin had suggested my inclusion and nudged my
nomination along.

Jeannie and I were twitchy about lifts and
often spoke as we ascended together to the
seventeenth floor of the UTS tower building in
Broadway, Sydney, reassuring each other with
distracting conversation. She introduced me to the
novels of Martin Cruz Smith (*Gorky Park*) and the
Swedish writers Maj Sjöwall and Per Wahlöö who
wrote the Martin Beck novels that a generation
later became the TV series *Beck*. Some refer to
them as the founders of Nordic Noir. They are
still on my bedroom bookshelves. Yes, I read in
bed. For the conference I wrote a narrative using
multiple voices, mostly those of people living with
HIV/AIDS at the time or people closely associated
with them. Lesley and I alternated in speaking the
voices. The paper owed much to discussions with
Jodi Brooks, Kathy Triffitt, Ken Davis, Jack Wallace,
and Ross Duffin, but the format was an experiment
in performing narrative theory: 'AIDS Narratives,
Gay Sex and the Hygienics of Innocence.' It was
a response to the NSW parliamentary inquiry
into compensation for 'innocent' victims of HIV
infection. That is, those who contracted it through
sex or needles were by implication 'guilty'.

The Perth paper was not the first time I had
spoken about HIV and AIDS, but it marked the
beginning of twenty years more. While still at UTS,
I began to work collaboratively with Gary Dowsett
on research projects at his invitation and in 1994

he and Susan Kippax, the Director of the National Centre in HIV/AIDS Social Research, invited me to do a plenary presentation at the Centre's annual national conference. My friend Kevin's then partner Robert Martin died about a week before I was due to speak. (I had introduced them five years before.) I had gone with Robert to the clinic three or four years before his death when he was tested for HIV and again ten days later when he received his diagnosis. We had sat in his car afterwards, talking for an hour or more. Kevin and I arranged the funeral. I spoke at it and I began to write the conference presentation the day after, a few days before it was due to be given. I spoke about the relations between love, death, gay men and the absence of both gay sex and HIV/AIDS in Mike Newell's 1994 film, *Four Weddings and a Funeral*. I suggested amongst other things that the absence of gay sex from the film was based on a calculation that the audience would see gay sex as HIV infectious sex. (Many of the non-gay characters were at it like rabbits, often hilariously.) This absence in turn enabled the representation of the love between the two gay men as true love. I suggested that the film used the funeral to explore the difference between officially sanctioned relationships and 'real' relationships. 1994 was the peak year of AIDS deaths in Australia. About 700 people died. Over 90% were gay men. A version of the paper was published in the anthology *Divertika* (1995).

Jodi, Leigh and I went on to co-edit the queer issue of *Media International Australia* in 1995 at the invitation of Liz Jacka who was then the editor.

1995 was a busy year. I became an Australia Council Writer in Residence at the AIDS Council of NSW (ACON) for three months, on leave from UTS. About seventy people came to the introductory session. I ran three writing groups, each of about twenty people. Each group met three times. Group sessions were three hours long and I met with individual participants. I also edited one participant's autobiography, which he later published. Several of the participants were seriously unwell. Forty-four of them contributed to a restricted circulation collection of their writing. Their confidentiality was paramount. Some were writing their lives for the first time. Others wrote fiction.

One man wrote 'this sojourn with the pen has been the best head job I've had for ages.'

Another used the phrase 'a poltergeist of stilettos.'

All these years later I find myself suddenly imagining those stilettos flying through the air and sticking heel first into the wall. Leigh told me that year of how after a close friend died a cup flew from the dish rack and smashed to the floor.

That year too I was finishing *A Guide to Gay and Lesbian Writing in Australia* and was a co-judge with Robert Dessaix of the *Outrage* short story competition.

The Writer in Residency project reconnected me with Ross, who invited me to participate in the advisory structure of the national Gay Education Strategies project at the Australian Federation of AIDS Organisations (AFAO). Ross introduced me to amongst others Alan Brotherton, the then President of the National Association of People Living with HIV/AIDS who in turn introduced me I think to Rob Lake. Both Alan and Rob came to Christmas dinner along with others in 1997. Maybe Ross too. I did individual capons for ten. I must have been mad. Christmas in Australia, eh. By then I lived in Surry Hills. Ross and Alan between them gave me a good education and opportunities to play a useful role. Through Alan I later met his partner Luke Cutler. I have a green bud vase that Luke made. He gave it to me when I visited them in Adelaide. Actually, he gave me two. One made by him and another by his former partner. They are the same height and similarly styled, though each has a different green glass stem emerging out of a heavier bulbous clear glass bubbled base. They are quietly piss elegant in what Marshall I am sure would call mid-century modern style.

Alan worked at the AIDS Council in Adelaide, as well as in Victoria and NSW. He also spent several years at the International HIV/AIDS Alliance in Britain, and at the International AIDS Society. When Alan died in Sydney of complications from melanoma in 2015, Bill O'Loughlin gave one of the eulogies and both Rob and I amongst others wrote obituaries. My last dinner with Alan, though I did not know it at the time, was at a restaurant on the first floor of the only remaining late Victorian arcade in Sydney, the Strand. Kane Race joined us after he finished teaching. It was a warm-hearted evening as we enjoyed the surrounds. The roof of the Arcade was splendidly lit.

In August 1999, Lesley invited Joan Nestle and I to create a session at the Melbourne Writers Festival on Sex and Death. I had admired Joan's writing for many years, especially *A Restricted Country* (1987) and *Sister and Brother* (1995), co-edited with John Preston, in which lesbians and gay men wrote about their lives together. Joan and I met in Mitch's backyard and began the process of creating a joint paper. We had both had cancers, both liked sex and were each deeply affected by the AIDS epidemic. We performed it, again with Lesley, in alternating voices. Joan was a key player in the formation of the Lesbian Herstory Archives in New York. She lives in Melbourne with her partner Di Otto and is a co-patron with Dennis Altman of the Australian Lesbian and Gay Archives. She has written extensively on lesbian sex and sexual politics. Leigh interviewed her in New York in 1994. Mitch as it happened was in the room. They were each there separately for the Gay Games.

It was around the time of the Writers Festival that I became Researcher in Residence in a joint project between AFAO and the Australian Research Centre in Sex, Health and Society (ARCSHS), Latrobe University. My AFAO manager was Alan, followed by Dermot Ryan. Good managers both. The first of several reports and working papers from that project, guided by Garrett Prestage, Michael Costello and Jon Willis, was on HIV treatments uptake amongst Indigenous gay community attached men in Sydney and Brisbane. It indicated that on the limited available data, treatments uptake was at similar levels to that of non-Indigenous urban gay men. That was good news. The report went at Jon's suggestion to the National Indigenous Australian Sexual Health Committee. He also prompted me to edit a collection of research papers from ARCSHS on cultures of care and safe sex amongst HIV Positive Australians.

As Researcher in Residence I collaborated closely with Levinia Crooks (1960–2017) at the Australian Society for HIV Medicine and Jo Watson at the National Association of People Living with HIV/AIDS. Levinia and Kirsty Machon were the last to leave my fiftieth birthday. I still have one of the two glass and green plastic coffee plungers Levinia bought at Peter's of Kensington for the party. They were on special. $5 each. She had insisted on doing the catering, though Kevin and Brett I think did the cake: white icing, a rainbow across one corner, 22cm candles, and another corner adorned by a glass humming bird. I have that too. I need to glue the flower that the bird was sipping from back on.

Leigh spoke and told funny rude stories. Close friends know detailed dirt. I giggled nervously throughout, but I doubt anyone there was all that surprised by what he said.

By then Leigh and I had been having breakfast most Saturdays in the old Metro Theatre building where thirty years earlier I had gone to see *Hair*. Leigh moved to Melbourne not long after my birthday. Two years later I went down to Melbourne to work at ARCSHS, 2001–2010. On my first day I met Marian Pitts who had come from England as the new Director and I worked again with Gary Dowsett and many others. In 2005, with Marian's support, testimonials from Gary and Terry Goldie in Canada and good supervision from Nicky Solomon and Andrew Jakubowicz at UTS I at long last completed a PhD. The three examiners were complimentary. No changes needed. I kept on talking. I didn't need a PhD to do that, but it helped in being heard.

In 2007, Marian and Anthony Smith invited me to write the last chapter in their book *Researching the Margins*. I was interested in how deficit configurations of 'marginality' might actually reproduce it. I asked instead how in the face of health and other deficits we might simultaneously acknowledge the powerful social capacities generated by the experiences of marginality – the voices of community resistance. I was following the work of Isaac Julian and Kobena Mercer. It is a matter of how we represent our various collective selves, and in the process reduce the risk of becoming hostages to tokenism. Who among us gets to speak? In what situations? We are not all the same.

The research work at ARCSHS and collaborations with the National HIV Centres were a long way from my degrees in Philosophy and

Australian Literature, and teaching in textual and cultural studies, but I liked multidisciplinary work for all its methodological challenges. If I locate myself anywhere in terms of a discipline it is in Cultural Studies. Sem(en)antics, one might say. My work with Garrett on intensive sex partying (2009), and the thinking I put into the monograph *Then and Now. Gay Men and HIV* (2003) come to mind, as does my retirement presentation 'When HIV is Endemic amongst Gay Men', published in 2011.

I knew Ken Davis and Ross from gay and left politics in the 1970s, along with many others: Phil Carswell, Gay Walsh, Laurie Bebbington, Margaret Lyons, Adam Carr, Steve Oram, Ken Howard, David Menadue, Graham, Paul Harris, Bruce Sims, Peter Ronge, Susan Ardill, Liz Ross, Alison Thorne to name only some. Every one of them has made their own often significant contributions to gay and lesbian lives. I think for example of Adam's early AIDS journalism in *Outrage*, his, Phil's and Alison's roles in the founding of the Victorian AIDS Council, David's book *Positive* (2003) and Bruce's role in editing and publishing gay and lesbian writing while at Penguin Australia. I have written about gay and lesbian life in Melbourne during the seventies elsewhere (Hurley 2015, 2011). Several of us are also '78ers who were there either on the night of the first Mardi Gras arrests or participated in subsequent demonstrations. Along with hundreds of others I was part of the march from the fourth national conference at Paddington Town Hall. About fifty of us were arrested at Taylor Square. I still have the arrest sheet. It too was in the name of Roger Casement.

The potted euphorbia Paul Harris gave me some years ago is going strong outside my back door, as is the tree hydrangea. In autumn its leaves are a rich russet red.

In spring I watch butterflies swirl in a purple haze of Buddleia.

I missed Kevin's seventieth. I was in Europe at the time. Moira and Louise were there. Kevin's partner Brett had written to invite me. I missed Mitch's sixtieth too for that matter, a few years before. I was away in Sydney for work.

At my own sixtieth I said amongst other things, 'I was not born into belonging.'

At Bruce Sims' and Peter Ronge's, in 2001, I meet Frank Prain over dinner. Frank tells me years later when we crossover in London, that we had met at the First National Homosexual Conference in August 1975. Perhaps we danced together. That weekend is somewhat blurred. I take him at his word. Dinner with these three has occurred many times. They share concert or opera tickets with me when one or the other can't go. I benefit from their generosity and enjoy their company.

Individual friendships often enough have their origins in political networks or overlapping friendship circles. They come from shared participation in activism. Several of my friends come from the period of the Philosophy Strike at Sydney University in 1973, the struggles over getting Political Economy as a course and student moves to democratise aspects of university life. I met Craig and Julie in 1973, and over the next weeks and months Liz Jacka and Toni Robertson and Wiebke and Gill Leahy and Christine Miles and a host of others. Wiebke tells me then about the Bauhaus, probably Toni did too. Toni was part of the Earthworks Collective. I had a framed set of her series of eight 'Taking Market Town by Strategy' posters (1976–1977) in which female shoppers organise to take-over a shopping complex. Last time I saw them they were on the walls of the house Kevin and Robert had bought in Sydenham, and quite possibly still are. I will ask Kevin and Brett. They are also in the Australian Print Collection of the National Gallery of Australia.

(I recently visited Keven and Brett. The posters are in their hall on the Central Coast.)

In Melbourne I lived in several shared houses for five years before moving to live alone in St Kilda, from 1980–1984. Jude Munro was the through line as each house reconstituted. She was an organiser. I was a dreamer wannabe, putting myself together, working fulltime, doing a Masters, active in my union. Jude and I have seen each other infrequently over the last thirty years. Her sixtieth at Virginia's was one occasion, but I knew where she was. In 2016 I was in Lyon, France, for a week. After I posted pics on Facebook a message popped up asking if I was still there. It was Jude. Coincidentally she was too. We met up, wandered the sights and had a great Sunday evening in a small jazz club listening to the locals play. I look at a map. Maybe the venue was La Clef de Voûte. Google translates it as The Keystone. We were easy companions. In the late 1970s we went occasionally to The Key Club in Gertrude St. Fitzroy, but that wasn't for jazz. Some nights were gay, some lesbian and others mixed. Disco and beer accompanied the pleasure of being in the company of our own kind.

I pause for a smoke, pull weeds from the midst of the low growing grevillea in the backyard that attracts small birds and think about accidental happy events.

I was part of the Melbourne response in the Greg Weir and Penny Short campaigns, the 1978 campaign against the visit of the British moralist Mary Whitehouse, and the defence of those arrested at the first Mardi Gras. Bruce and Peter invited me to join the Gay Trade Unionists Group. I became an organiser and participant in the 1981 national Homosexuality and Socialism conference in Melbourne. Graham, Phil and I engaged in public discussions of 'Which Way Forward for Australian Gays' published in the 1981/1982 Summer edition of *International Socialist*. Like others, we were each going our own ways politically. (For more context on these matters read Liz Ross' *Revolution Is for Us: The Left and Gay Liberation in Australia*). During that time, I began to withdraw from movement activism as the realities of fulltime work, fulltime postgraduate study and active unionism bit hard. Undiagnosed depression did not help. Commitment was one thing, knowing how to manage its demands another. I took to board games – Risk, Mahjong, Diplomacy – for relaxation, read a lot of Robert Ludlum and slumped further into melancholy with Edward Upward's *No Home but the Struggle* (1977). I was uplifted much more recently by reading that at age ninety-two Upward began an eight-year sexual relationship with a woman forty-six years younger. He died in 2009, aged 105.

In the later 1980s, when we were both in Sydney, Jan McKemmish had introduced me to Helen Barnes. They had met at the Belvoir Theatre. Helen and I shared pots of tea for many months in 1989 and, thirty years later, still do, though now it is mostly coffee.

I met Moira Carmody in 1975 through Richard Riley in the student bar at UNSW and we became close friends. In late 1995, Richard took the photo of me that appears on the page opposite the title page of the *Guide*. In October 2017, I was Bridesman at the wedding of Moira and Louise in the British Consulate, in Sydney, with a view of the Bridge and Opera House. I had spoken at her fiftieth birthday in the Blue Mountains about ten years earlier. It was there I met Louise. Both Moira and Mitch had separately put me onto Armistead Maupin's *Tales of the City* novels. One of the things Moira and I did was go to exhibitions together when she was in Melbourne: Bowie, Jean-Paul Gaultier, Viktor and Rolf. Moira likes a handbag.

Moira died in February 2020. There was a large red self-standing handbag on her coffin. In mid 2017 she had emailed me. She was in Sydney and I was in Berlin: 'I wish you were here to talk to, but I think there will be much to come when you return.' There was.

Through Lesley, I met Garrett Prestage in 1978 who over time became a good friend and still is, along with his partner Trevor. They are the only people who can get me to go to a musical – sometimes. Gentle but persistent pressure is applied, and I am outflanked by kindness. To my surprise I enjoyed *Abba* and *Jersey Boys*. I then recall I have also seen *Chicago* twice, but Jimmy Chi's *Bran Neu Dae* is far and away my favourite musical. I saw it first at the Seymour Centre in the early nineties. Initially I think I went with Chrissie Miles but maybe not. More likely it was with my then boyfriend. From 2000 on, Garrett gave me opportunities that made the last decade of my working life much more productive than it may have been. We catch up whenever one of us is in the other's city and have also done so in London and Berlin.

I have lived much of my adult life sustained by these networks of friends and colleagues, by lovers and the pleasures of random strangers and friends with benefits. They still sustain me. Objects in my cabinet tell me so, though they are not the full story, if such exists at all. If it does, it's not finished yet.

I use the word lover despite its ambiguities.

Sometimes the ice is thin. One pirouettes, waiting for the cracking sound.

I once asked a friend, an eminent professor whose research is of considerable international

repute, a question about how she saw herself.
She said she was a 'journeyman'. A journeyman
is a certified, skilled, authorised worker in a
trade or craft who is employed on the basis of
demonstrated capacity in using those skills. She
would be very unlikely to refer to herself as a
scholar or an intellectual or a theorist. It was a
chastening moment for me who much of the time
had wanted to be recognised as one or more of
these. Now she and I drink coffee together in cafes,
mostly Tin Pot in North Fitzroy, or sometimes tea
in her garden. We talk of books and politics and
mutual friends. It is time I called her and took the
teapot out of the cabinet.

I might add that this friend of mine, speaks
and reads French fluently. To my embarrassment,
I do neither. I have no second language much
less a third or a fourth. French was compulsory in
first form (Year 7) at Albury High in 1962, but the
class was large, the will was lacking, and French
was foreign in the sense of alien. I had little sense
of modernity other than milking machines and
little of internationality, as distinct from English
connections. French had no apparent use value.
It was spoken on the other side of the world, but
not in England, and the only channels I knew of
were for crop irrigation. The worst thing you could
possibly be was different. 'Oui, Monsieur' made us
snigger. (The birth of a yobbo. I still have traces.) But
regimes of nationally and regionally inflected taste
and refinement were starting to clash. Nor did I have
much formal understanding of the parts of speech
or grammar. I learned that in Latin in subsequent
years and door-knocked our army neighbours,
mostly the Catholics, trying to find someone who
might be able to help me understand what my
homework required. Their incomprehension was
good-willed, my desire for sense often unsatisfied.

Without knowing it, I was on a very slow journey out of what I had known so far.

It wasn't only my own provincialism that began to shift. Australia, too, well parts of it, was slowly changing in the face of the long-term social and political struggles of Aboriginals and Torres Strait Islanders. In 1962, the Menzies government's *Commonwealth Electoral Act of 1962* granted Indigenous people the right to vote in federal elections. In 1966, the Holt government passed a new migration act that established formal equality between British, European and non-European immigrants. A year later Aboriginal people were granted the right to be counted in the census. As conservative as I was still, I began to learn things about Australia that didn't sit easily with a slowly emerging sense of social justice. I became increasingly aware of the Vietnam War. A teacher tore down the anti-conscription poster on the door of the study three of us shared at the school hostel. I was climbing The Rock between Culcairn and Henty the day Harold Holt died swimming in rough seas off Portsea Beach. It was December 17, 1967, the year I finished high school.

Life writing has standard forms – memoir, autobiography, diaries, profiles, profiling, arrest sheets, clinical notes – and deviations.

What is the point of being a deviant if you do not deviate?

I am not the first to consider how Barthes' homosexuality bore down on his writing, much less his living. Once his literary executor published *Incidents,* the question was discussed for over a decade.

I knew this but had not thought about it for perhaps thirty years until I found myself reading Sontag again on Barthes. As I read, I made a mental note to check what if anything Ross Chambers had said in his *Loiterature* (1999) or elsewhere. It was then that I remembered too, D.A. Miller's *Bringing Out Roland Barthes* (1992).

Miller brings out Barthes in much the same way as I bring a cup out of the cabinet. He puts Barthes into view, as an object of curiosity, a site of affection, a source of fascination. His interest is in the theoretical relations that emerge in doing so, and the opportunities these provide for intellectual play in writing that proposes an 'album of moments ... a classificatory disturbance.'

Miller wrote from deep within the shadows of the AIDS epidemic in the USA – the homophobia of the murderous response under Reagan and his creation of ongoing 'culture wars.' His interest in Barthes' sexuality was in how it could be used to alleviate '*an erotic pessimism*' by producing with him, against him, a sexuality that had become 'ours'. He staged an imaginary relation, using Barthes' writing to investigate what it meant to put one's body on the line and between the lines. By then Barthes was ten years dead. Miller asked

> who could ever think– in particular, at this date, what gay man–that someone's death ever stopped the elaboration of someone else's fantasies about him?

I was in New York briefly the year *Bringing Out Roland Barthes* was published. The day before I landed, Madonna released her *Erotica* album. Hours after I reached Manhattan, she was launching her book of erotic photos, *Sex*. It was encased in aluminium, wrapped in polyester film and became the fastest selling coffee-table book of all time. On the same night there was an AIDS Coalition to Unleash Power (ACT UP) action at St Patrick's Cathedral. Police and ambulance

sirens sped up Sixth Avenue, and I discovered
the Limelight Club. Miller asserted a sexuality
that had become ours against erotic pessimism.
Classificatory disturbances at the Limelight were
the *soup de nuit*.

Many gay men asserted sexual pleasure despite
being surrounded by death and disease. Safe sex,
including condoms, sero-sorting between HIV-
positive men and negotiated safety between HIV-
negative men, initially made that possible. Miller
was being playful as well as serious. Twenty-five
years after he wrote, I am momentarily re- entering
this fantasy relation though my own relations with
what is often being represented now as mainstream
gay have shifted around somewhat. The majority of
gay identifying men now do not know anyone who
died of AIDS. I am glad of that, though it is not my
experience. I am even more glad that people I know
are still alive.

'Ours' has more dimensions for me than just
HIV. That is probably true of all my friends including
those who live with HIV and have made lives
both with it and despite it. The social conventions
embedded in many current accounts of ordinary
life – access to IVF, engagements, marriages,
children, family – increasingly became the major
public vectors of struggles for legal equality after
the election of the Howard government in 1996.
That is now quite a time ago, but it depends when
you are looking from. I came out in 1972 and was
sexually active before that. I had learned to live
my life as a gay man despite what the state said I
could and could not do legally, though of course
I was at times cautious. The first twelve+ years of
my sex life in Victoria and NSW were illegal, except
when I visited South Australia after 1975. Tasmania
legalised homosexuality in 1997. My luck held out
in the meantime. Not everyone's did. Illegality is

still the case in many countries. Like others at the time, especially in the 1970s, I did not ask the state for personal validation and still do not. Nor did I expect it. Many of us made our own way and treated the state with disdain if not hostility. Most of us still have a critical relation with its actions and policies even when we support the governing party to whatever degree we do and insist on civil rights and legal equality. We're not alone in making demands on officialdom while continuing on with our own social collectivities and sexual mores.

My early experiences of out gay life were more to do with the forms of social activity that accompanied politics rather than bar life: dinners (out, and in), pubs, parties, dances. That did not really change much for me until 1987 when bars, sex venues and dance parties became recreation central.

I have had several romantic relationships in my time, but I have never wanted to be a parent and have no personal interest in marrying. Several of my lesbian, gay, bi and heterosexual friends are parents with children from previous or current relationships, whether formalised as marriages or not. I have episodically changed nappies, baby sat, watched children grow up, eaten with them at dinner tables, and sometimes mentored or been of educational assistance, coached. They have grown up with me in the mix. No doubt I have also irritated and bored them on occasion. Remembering these matters has prompted me to consider how my thinking changes in the face of shifting realities, but not always. Like many others, I voted for equality not for marriage. Much more importantly, from my point of view, well before then I had stopped being moralistic about other people's choices. Others may query that remark, but I have been an official witness at weddings several times.

173

The tenderness I seek is surely my own, and I work on it, but often enough it comes through interaction with others. One adapts, sometimes well, sometimes badly, gets stuck, moves on, changing one's relations with one's self. Or not.

As I score these memories in my writing, prompted and entranced as I am by the charms of porcelain, and the shine of electroplated silver, I realise how much these communal friendships have carried, nurtured, protected, surrounded and encouraged me. It is here in personal relations my sense of community is now felt most strongly, yet activism, community organisations, workplaces, and lived cultures one way or another run through these connections, providing structure, social possibility and quality of life. That experience was and is 'ours'. I find it impossible to imagine how I might have lived as I did and do without it.

Necessity is often challenging when the circumstances are not of one's own choosing. Others among my friends might say they always wanted, or have come to want, a version of conventional family life. What is clear is that we have been and are creative in our personal lives and are a much more heterogeneous lot than was evident in the marriage debate. 'Ours' in this sense is a multi-hued achievement.

Reading Miller again, I am reminded again and again of the struggles in that first decade of death and destruction against those who used a virus to reinstall homophobia with great viciousness. It happened across the world, and still does. As I write homosexuality is still illegal in 41 of the 53 Commonwealth countries. While homophobia may turn out to be in its last gasp, it also may not. In Australia it is still happening if somewhat unevenly around religiously driven discrimination, false and malicious attacks on the safe schools programme, sex education, sex research and on the sex and gender politics of trans.

Miller 'brings out' Barthes in an imaginary homosexual encounter. Cruising down Memory Lane I repeat this motif. Strangers to many each may be, yet for me both men are 'ours.' Memories of how they engaged with what matters to me here bring a forgotten fondness, a re-flowering of interest that I put to purpose.

Barthes' *Incidents* is a relatively slight book, a relief in some ways. It contains four pieces, two not previously published. One of those two, the title piece 'Incidents', is a collection of notes. Each note is a sentence or two or three of observations of life in Morocco. Ross Chambers calls them 'storyless points.' Barthes writes,

> A delicate, almost gentle, boy, his hands already a little coarse, suddenly makes the triggerlike gesture that reveals the young punk: flicking the ash off his cigarette with the back of a fingernail.

As one can see the observations are not neutral. Any story there might be could be made from the tonal style. A story of what Barthes saw when he looked – 'almost' gentle, a 'little' coarse, suddenly, triggerlike, reveals, 'young punk', flicking the ash – is a story of a specific if minimalist body and its gestures. For Chambers in *Loiterature*, this method is a counting out, a 'telling' in the sense of an enumeration, but I would add, a telling one at that. For there is delight here too, in the adjectivally modified observations – along with acuity. We are one step away from a scene in Jean Genet's novels or stylised French gangster films. Calvet tells us Barthes had long kept index cards with notes on them, but his prose elsewhere was often also dense, sometimes elliptical and conceptually complex for a reader not already immersed in his ways of thinking.

Chambers also suggests that in 'Incidents' Barthes presents a euphemised sexual hunting posing as 'touristic curiosity', whereas in the essay 'Soiree de Paris' we see 'a kind of defeated diffidence'. He goes on to discuss possible relations between race, racism and gay male desire in sexual tourism. He asks,

> What incidences link the commoditised erotic relations that are so prominent in the cruisy Parisien text with the striking deemphasis of commoditisation in the touristic Moroccan text?

Chambers' interest is in the repression of colonialism in Barthes' texts. It is this he argues that produces the sense of melancholic defeat Barthes voices in 'Soiree de Paris'. Barthes, he says, forgets the social context and that makes things seem pointless. That is the point of the stories. These are tough standards. Context is all. It is an elaborate nuanced discussion over several pages and my summary does not do the elaboration justice.

It is the phrase 'defeated diffidence' which interests me. Chambers clearly thought it had no place in public writing or needed more analysis if it did. He blames 'the post-colonial illusion' for Barthes 'yielding to the banality of allowing personal misery to displace the consciousness one might expect of a critical intellectual.'

Cruising is enticing, often a delight, but is also not always rewarding. Sometimes it can be done as a way of mediating other feelings, often enough without one knowing immediately what the feelings are but wanting to get away from oneself.

IV

Some people watch films on that basis, or garden. Others cruise, sometimes diffidently. I can hear the Shirelles singing, 'Mama said there'll be days like this.' Van Morrison's 'Days like this' is different. Between them they cover the bases. There are days things go fine. And days they don't.

Dorothy Porter wrote in her poem 'Faith':

> other times
> have left me
> stranded and sobbing
> in a muggy black night
> of longing
> and plain bloody nonsense
>   (in *other worlds*, 2001)

I met Ross Chambers a couple of times in about 2009 and we corresponded briefly about an article he was writing. He died in October 2017. In 2014, Meaghan Morris credited him with 'transforming literary theory into an urgent, difficult practice of cultural thought about the politics of "poetics" in life.' In particular she singled out his books *Facing It: AIDS Diaries and the Death of the Author* (1998) 'and a magnificent book on the material effects of atrocity and witnessing in history, *Untimely Interventions: AIDS Writing, Testimonial and the Rhetoric of Haunting* (2004).'

I began reading Barthes perhaps in 1982. I found him hard going for a year or five. In hindsight that doesn't surprise me. I have, however, engaged with his thought on and off ever since. I was a tie-dyed Althusserian Marxist before that, also beginning to engage with Foucault, and hearing of Kristeva, Irigaray, Cixous, and Lyotard. At least when translated, French intellectuals were not totally foreign to me. My Philosophy honours thesis in 1974 relied in large part on Althusser, Poulantzas, and women's and gay liberation. It is not that I couldn't read hard stuff, but switching from that specific intellectual frame, with Raymond Williams, E.P. Thompson, Ralph Miliband and *New Left Review* running alongside, to Barthes and Foucault was just plain challenging. They were often, as we used to say, incommensurable. That was the point. Conceptual frameworks challenge each other.

It did not help that also in 1982 I was doing a preliminary year for a Master's degree in Australian Literature. and had my first melanoma. AIDS was just on the horizon. Five years later in 1987 the melanoma came back and required a second, and more major, operation. It threw me off kilter. I learned a bit about meditation to manage anxiety and sometimes went chanting with Ken Davis, Fabian lo Shiavo and others. Support takes many forms. I was held as they say, often metaphorically but also on occasion literally. I had met Fabian both at Ken and Paul van Reyk's various soirees – a Karen Black video afternoon anyone? – and earlier at national homosexual conferences. (I play Cesaria Evora's CD 'Sodade', a later gift from Ken, as I write.) Fabian was a key player in conference workshops where religious matters were discussed. I could not understand putting gay and Christianity together and made sectarian anti-religious interventions. I still don't understand, but over several conferences Fabian's polite friendly steadiness, kindness and commitment to a radical gay politics made me reassess my behaviour. One time he was absent, and I realised I missed him. I knew I had to change – the problem was mine, not him as a person. Secularly speaking, the gay left is a broad church. Fabian has had several, sometimes simultaneous, personas including being Mother Abbyss of Sydney's Sisters of Perpetual Indulgence, U.S. evangelist Reverend Oral Riches and as mentioned earlier Monsignor

Porca Madonna. Unsurprisingly, he liked a good chant too.

At the time the melanoma returned, the death rate from AIDS was rising steadily. It hit hard amongst my friends, friends of friends, social networks.

In 1992, Bill O'Loughlin and I were both pall bearers at Ken 'Joe' McClelland's funeral in Melbourne. Bill gave the eulogy. Ken had first introduced us briefly in the mid 1980s. Ross Duffin re-introduced Bill and I again in the mid 1990s, on the day Bill was farewelled as the President of the Australian Federation of AIDS Organisations. A year or so after, Ross, Alan and I came down to Melbourne from Sydney for Bill's fortieth. I gave Bill some water-iris rhizomes. Rose and Mitch and other friends were also there. It was a big backyard party. It is time I re-potted the water iris that came back to me about fifteen years later when Bill moved flats and no longer had a garden.

Bill likes the paintings of Caravaggio. As do I, although I do not have his trained eye for technique. For one of his birthdays I wrote a poem that included the stanzas,

> Moving along we might note together
> the right nipple in the scarlet drama
> of a young John the Baptist
> half risen from sleep in the wilderness
> and the head-down, snuffling shadowy beast
>
> > 'the roughened, sunburnt hands
> > and neck of a labourer...who
> > has gotten undressed for his
> > modelling session.'
>
> even as we ask what woke the lad.
> ...

In St Jerome, the quill and the sinewy muscle of age
but not the paperweight skull
work hard
     against the dark.
Below the books, a cloth hangs,
somewhat extraneously,
in a formally folded sharp white vee.
Miss Scarlett in the library
ignores Colonel Mustard.

> 'In the room the women come and go
> Talking of Michelangelo.'

There's no through line in culture
except we make it so.

I spent twenty-one years of my life speaking, researching and writing publicly about gay men, HIV, people living with HIV/AIDS, social aspects of HIV treatments cultures, grief, sex, safe sex, risky sex, ecstatic sex. I did so mostly in an Australian context, but also sometimes overseas. I was an invited member of an International Gay Men's Health Thinktank which met in San Francisco, London and Sydney, 2001–2002. There were 20–30 of us involved in the different meetings. In San Francisco I spoke about anal sex and where and how it figures in health and pleasure. Years later Paul Kidd and Brent Allan reminded me that I spoke of the dribbling joys of eating ripe plums. I was arsing about with metaphors. I think that was where I first met Will Nutland, but I may have met him before that. He went on to become a co-founder of the activist group Prepster and a major mover in the promotion of pre-exposure prophylactic drugs (PrEP) that prevent HIV. Will warms my heart. PrEP has significantly reduced the number of new HIV infections in countries where it is available.

Will, Brent and Eric Rofes had organised
the Thinktank. I had met Eric when we spoke at
Health in Difference, the First National Lesbian
Gay Transgender and Bisexual Health Conference
in Sydney in October 1996. Ross Duffin had played
a major role in initiating it. I have written sexual
fiction and explicit health promotion stories
and spoken openly about what various gay men
do sexually in many places, but not here in this
writing to the regret of more than one pre-reader. I
discussed this recently with Ross. If it does not fit,
Michael, he said, it does not fit.

Some of us from the Thinktank met again
in November 2005 in Paris at a conference in the
Hotel de Ville organised by Warning, a breakaway
group from ACT-UP Paris. The conference was
intended to create a space for discussion of new
ideas on the relations between living gay lives,
HIV prevention and health – 'HIV and Gay Health.
New concepts, new approaches.' It was snowing
the morning I arrived after the long flight from
Australia and wonderful to be on the streets of the
Marais as I waited for my hotel room to be ready. I
got colder and colder as more snow fell and realised
my romance with the side streets off the Rue de
Rivoli was putting me at risk. I needed to retreat
indoors. On my first visit in early 1988 I had stayed
on the Left Bank and had extended discussions
about Baldwin in a bar with a straight English guy
whose parents had come from the Caribbean about
the time I had left with mine for Australia. I was
in full flight. On the third night there he began
to avoid me. I wandered off to the Tuileries and
felt the thickness of worsted serge trousers under
a woollen coat. He said something. I slurred a
fractured 'je ne parlais pas Francais' in response.
He too moved to avoid me. I walked back to my
room at about 2am along the Seine. What seemed

like gaslight on poles from a century earlier guided my way through the mist.

That first night in 2005 I met Olivier Jablonski, Georges Sideris and Sylvie Nadia Rouby, activists, intellectuals and conference organisers. We ate Chinese as I nodded off with jetlag through thick accents and constant translations in both directions. My head spun.

The crossover people from the Thinktank included amongst others Eric Rofes from San Francisco, Chris Bartlett from Philadelphia, and Will, Peter Keogh and others from London. I also met Tony Valenzuela and his partner Rob from LA. I had great respect for Tony's work as an HIV-positive activist who wasn't afraid to talk about sex, sex work, drugs and barebacking. Tony's speeches and articles in *Poz* magazine had outraged many, including members of ACT-UP Paris. As he was speaking on the first day of the Paris conference one of their activists emptied a bag of HIV pharmaceuticals in front of him in protest. His refusal to moralise was being blamed for new infections. Eric was one of Tony's few early public defenders. Tony recently stepped down after nine years as Executive Director of Lambda Literary, the leading LGBTQ literary organisation in the USA.

As glamorous as speaking in the Hotel de Ville might seem, and I was thrilled to be there, we were in a rabbit warren of prefabricated rooms on the lower level. One of the opening speakers was Jean-Luc Roméro, the first gay politician to be outed in France, and the first to reveal he was HIV positive. Romero had been outed in the gay press in 2000 and sued the journalist. He began to speak. The next speaker scheduled to come after Romero was Didier Eribon, then known as an author of books on several matters, including *Insult and the Making of the Gay Self* (1999), now an eminent professor. He had been critical of the suing of the journalist. He began interrupting Romero. This occurred several times. There was much volubility. Civility was stretched thin. The audience grew restive. Eribon persisted, deaf to remonstrance, and then gave his own address. By the time Olivier rose to speak, time for the morning session was considerably constrained. Four more of us were lined up waiting: me, Eric, Will and Rommel Mendès-Leite. In deference to the following speakers and the time, I did what one does, summarised as I went, shortened on the fly. That's the way these things sometimes go.

The proceedings of the conference were later published in a book *Santé Gaie* (Gay Health) under the direction of Olivier, Jean-Yves le Talec and Georges. Olivier had translated my presentation into French and included it. The boy who still could not speak French, now could not read his own published work. I had arrived very happily in a foreign place. My chagrin is a separate matter.

At that time Graham Willett was teaching Australian Studies units at the Free University of Berlin and came to Paris after the conference for a catch up before I returned to Australia. I have a photo of him that I took with my back to the old Opera House. Behind Graham is a BNP bank building. In the photo the street level façade of the building is covered with a breathtaking large leafed green nouveau vine with red flowers in the top left and right corners. It frames and decorates the doorway. In 2013 I met up with Cahal in Paris and took him to see the vine. It was no longer there. It had been moved elsewhere and I could no longer find it.

As we walked round the back of the opera house, I showed Cahal a plaque celebrating

Diaghelev who began the Ballets Russes with
productions there, but that is another story.

A day or two after, I introduced Cahal to Olivier
and Georges. They invited us to lunch at their
home. I have a photo of Olivier on his motorbike
talking with Cahal on the street like two local guys
meeting in passing, *les mecs*.

In 2016, I was staying in Oberkampf for a week
around the corner from the Bataclan theatre, one of
the scenes of major terrorist attacks in the previous
November. Ninety people had died. There were still
guards outside the theatre. Olivier, Georges and I
met at the Gare de Montparnasse and caught the
train to Chartres. Olivier and I talked non-stop all
the way there and almost all the way back. Catch
up time. We wandered through the town, spent an
hour in the Cathedral and wandered more. Georges
cooked dinner. He can be a lively polemicist, and
sometimes a fierce conversationalist, even, if
necessary, from two rooms away. We laugh a lot. I
have now eaten at their table several times. Georges
is a historian of the Byzantine period. His PhD
thesis was on eunuchs and power. Olivier says it is
monumental. The book is coming. I must ask how
it goes. They too travel. The second last time I saw
them was in Berlin where we ate Japanese. Café
Berio was too crowded. I cannot hear in noise.

It is quite a while now since I have seen
Chris Bartlett in person, ten years or more. He
is Executive Director of the William Way LGBT
Community Centre in Philadelphia. We last saw
each other at a GLBTI Health conference there in
2007. Eric had died suddenly not that long before.
Chris, I and others spoke at a memorial session.
Olivier, Georges, Sylvie and Tony were also present
as was Tony. The day before the conference
began, Chris took me to Tony's hotel room in the
conference venue. Tony was being interviewed

by a young postgraduate student Trevor Hoppe. I had met Trevor briefly in San Francisco at the time of the first Thinktank meeting. He went on to co-edit *The War on Sex* with David Halperin (2017) and published *Punishing Disease. HIV and the Criminalisation of Sickness* in 2018. At the conference, I presented on the work I had been doing with Garrett on intensive sex partying. It went down well. Trevor contacted me in 2015 to say his friend, Andrew Brown, and Andrew's partner Chris Ahrens were coming from the USA to live in Melbourne and could I meet with them. I did. Many dinners and brunches have followed. I introduced them in turn to Dino Hodge. We eat, laugh, gossip, share knowledges, play Cards against Humanity, create mutuality. New friendships, new times.

In the café of the hotel where the Philadelphia conference was held, I met Marshall Feldman, an Australophile who then lived in San Francisco. Marshall had been an AIDS social worker first at the AIDS Project of LA then for many years on one of LA's main AIDS wards at Cedars-Sinai Medical Centre, He had met several Australians, several of whom I also know, at American AIDS social work conferences. We had much to talk about. On subsequent visits to San Francisco, I would contact Marshall and we would meet for dinners and walks. On my last visit he offered to take me to the airport for my flight home. Alongside my hotel was a shop with a green fruit platter in the window that I pointed out and said how much I liked it. It is, says Marshall in a much later skype conversation, freeform mid-century-modern in style: 'It's high end, a good piece of glass. Like many mid-century pieces it is amorphous in form, referencing among other things a propeller.' It curves down to a lower middle rather than being flat, so though I call it a platter Marshall calls it a bowl. At the time I first saw it I had as usual dithered about buying it and when he came to pick me up the shop was shut. I'll get it and send it to you he said. I gave him the money and he did. That must have been about 2008 or so. Marshall has visited here twice since then and we travelled in Europe together in 2016. I introduced him to Leigh and Winston and he in turn entertained them in LA and they him here. The platter sits next to an elegant slim green glass jug that I bought in Darlinghurst, Sydney, in 1999. It seems it too is mid-century-modern. The two pieces sit on a sideboard. At the righthand end of the sideboard is a solid, rough edged lump of industrial glass, also green. It is a piece of detritus left over from smelting. I like the contrast with that of the refined glass.

My formal work in the HIV field largely stopped when I retired. Many began it much earlier than I, did much more, and some are doing it still. They have my respect. One way or another we responded together. That experience was accompanied by extraordinary moments and years of camaraderie: mutual trust, shared purpose, collective determination. These words barely scratch the surface of what people did and do for others.

We learned from each other: in formal and informal meetings, in whispers before we entered the rooms of the dying, on dance floors, in venues of the night, in cars and cafes, in days of workshopping, in accidental meetings on street corners. We listened, observed, reacted, responded, vented, were calm, focussed, insightful, sad, angry, grief struck, distracted and determined. There was a 'we' and an 'I' involved. Often enough there was a 'them' as well.

William Yang's photograph of a paper mache model of evangelist Fred Nile's head on a Carmen

Miranda-esque fruit platter, accompanied by the Sisters of Perpetual Indulgence, at the 1989 Sydney Gay and Lesbian Mardi Gras parade still gives me glee. I was there and delighted to see it. Wilde's Salome had set a fine example.

One of my major forms of relief in those days starting in 1985 was a weekly or fortnightly game of bridge. Ken Charnock and Steve McDonald taught Kevin and me how to play. Over the years, the players changed. Steve dropped out. Ken died. Jan H. and I dedicated *Two Timing* to him. He had said, 'get on with it.' I think of David Findlay, and of Roger Shaw who played with us. Roger also died. Liz and Christine and Shirley Dean became stalwarts. Peter Stevens did too for some years. Cathryn Garrigan joined us and Marion who moved to Wagga but played when in Sydney finishing her degree. Ross played very occasionally, as did June Crawford and Sue Kippax. A few months after I returned to Melbourne in 2001, Shirley, Chrissie and Liz came down and we played all through the Easter weekend, breaking only to eat, sleep, walk, and catch up on our separate lives. They continued playing in Sydney. On relatively regular work visits to Sydney, my bridge friends included me. Sunday nights at Liz's or Chrissie's or Shirley's. My game had deteriorated. I needed constant instruction. Deaths from AIDS had fallen dramatically. We breathed out. I wrote about that too. The pleasure in being with old friends intensified, even as Liz, Shirley and I worried about the advancing effects of Chrissie's Parkinson's disease.

Across the 1990s, I also wrote and spoke about gay and lesbian writing and publishing in Australia. It was my forte on and off for over twenty years. I began to develop it systematically in my teaching at UTS and in talks at Mardi Gras festival events from the late 1980s onwards. Those lectures and talks informed my invited Introduction to the student produced anthology *Pink Ink. An Anthology of Australian Lesbian and Gay Writers* (1991). Dorothy Porter launched the anthology at the Wicked Women's Warehouse in Chippendale. I was already a fan of her work. By then I was half way through writing *A Guide to Gay and Lesbian Writing in Australia* (1996). I dedicated it to 'the living and amongst the dead Ken 'Joe' McClelland.' I was chuffed to discover recently that it was still in over 130 international libraries.

Paul van Reyk emceed the Sydney launch of the *Guide* on the mezzanine of the State Theatre in Sydney during Mardi Gras, 1996. The cabaret and opera singer, and actor, Judi Connelli did the launching. Paul was dressed as 'Prissy' the maid from the film *Gone with the Wind*, originally played by Butterfly McQueen. I was very nervous about this in terms of how it might be received. Like me, Paul comes from an immigrant family and grew up in army camps. Unlike me he came from Sri Lanka. His emceeing was a virtuoso performance of race politics using camp, drag and bad taste in the interests of entertainment, while relying on the colour of his skin to get away with it – 'I can do it, you can't.' It was a tight rope balancing act that put the politics of racism firmly and clearly into the event. The first entry in the *Guide* is 'Aboriginal Gay and Lesbian Writing'.

The *Guide* was launched in both Sydney and Melbourne. Mitch was at the Sydney launch, as well as Melbourne. I wore the Gaultier jacket at both events with a gardenia in the lapel. There's a small pic in William Yang's *Friends of Dorothy* (1997). The stripes on the jacket came up fabulously in the glorious black and white photos taken by Mazz of Mazz Images in Sydney.

IV

There are gems in the tiara of everyday life.

The launch in Melbourne was held in South Yarra at Hares and Hyenas, courtesy of the owners Roland Thomson and Crusader Hillis. Annamarie Jagose did the launching. Initially I think Graham Willett emceed. Mitch thinks he may have too. Graham has no memory of doing so. I have a photo of Graham Carbery looking down at notes in his hand. I suspect he also spoke, if not indeed emceed.

The *Guide* was co-published by Allen and Unwin and the Australian Lesbian and Gay Archives (ALGA). Elizabeth Weiss, then at A&U. proved to be a warm hearted, generous, thoughtful editor. Graham Carbery (1947–2017) founded the Archives and he and Mitch played central roles in the publishing of the *Guide*. The Archives had published Graham's *A History of the Gay and Lesbian Mardi Gras* the year before. Mitch and Graham C. had both been members of the Gay Teachers and Students Group in Melbourne and Graham C. had been the public spokesperson for *Young, Gay and Proud* (1978).

Later in the year of the *Guide*'s launch, Mardi Gras asked me to write the introduction to an anthology they produced in tandem with Random House as distributors, *Fruit Salad. Salad. A Compote of Contemporary Gay and Lesbian writing*, edited by Trish Luker and Neal Drinnan. They then invited me to speak at the launch as part of the 1997 Mardi Gras festival. Random distributed 11,000 free copies to major bookshops nationally. The status of queers and their writing was changing rapidly. At the invitation of Graeme Aitken in 2002 I wrote about this in his edited collection, *The Penguin Book of Gay Australian Writing*.

I have written somewhat sparingly of such matters here. I seem to have wandered instead, strayed afield, entertained other selves I barely knew were there. Foucault put it this way:

> After all, what would be the value of the passion for knowledge if it resulted only in a certain amount of knowledgeableness and not, in one way or another and to the extent possible, in the knower's straying afield of himself?

I have enjoyed the straying. In the process, I collect myself.

Kevin and I gave Mitch a large Villeroy and Bosch plate for her fortieth in 1994. It sits on display in hers and Rose's kitchen, occasionally moving around as things are rearranged. We bought it in Myer. Mitch says Kevin said she was lucky to get it: 'Michael thought it cost too much.' The plate is decorated with an abstract design a la Russian constructivism: orange and black geometric shapes, solid black dots, fine black lines, spaced in clock style on a white background and all carefully positioned to achieve an overall balance. It is number two in a set of four. On the back the designer's name is given as Wladimir Njemuchin. Njemuchin is spelled differently elsewhere as Nemukhin (1925–2016). It seems I spoke at the birthday dinner, but I have neither memory nor notes on what it was I said. I also spoke at Mitch's and Rose's private commitment ceremony a decade later. I cannot find that speech right now either, but I know I have it. I sang a line: 'Love me tender. Love me true. All my dreams come true.' Given I cannot sing in tune with any reliability it was a risky move. It worked, just. If pushed, I prefer the Nicolas Cage version in David Lynch's *Wild at Heart* (1990.)

Kane Race has suggested there is not much point sharply opposing 'pleasures of self-confirmation and pleasures of self-disruption, *plaisir* and *jouissance*.' He suggests we instead look at events in which the two meet up and produce 'new objects, identities and ways of relating to the world.' I like that. Kane simply says let us see what we make of these varieties of pleasure when we investigate what it is gay men say and do in the process of making gay lives, especially but not only in their relations with sex and drugs.

My drug days are very long gone, unless we speak of blood thinners, anti-cholesterol lipids, blood pressure pills, anti-anxiety medication and more for reflux and gastritis. Oh, and for the last five years or so PrEP of course. It prevents HIV infection. I could riff here on ageing as a conjunctural event involving emerging relations with the self and others – did I just hear someone say Daddy? – but I am distracted by a more recent set of remarks from Kane. He discusses a 1976 Frank Thring advertisement for Martin cigarettes. Thring (1926–1994) appeared regularly on stage, television and in film, including the blockbusters *Ben Hur* (1959), *King of Kings* (1961), and *Mad Max. Beyond Thunderdome* (1985). I saw him sometimes on the streets of Melbourne in the seventies, wearing his signature loose black clothing. He was a distinctive figure with a distinctive manner.

The Martin's ad parodies Hollywood's idea of glamour, with a kind of fancy trash camp. Thring comes down a curved stairway, flanked by showgirls. He's wearing a glittering shiny suit. Under it is a ruffled shirt. A nod to Liberace perhaps. On the one hand we have a fetishised commodity, cigarettes, on the other a kind of studied theatrical nonchalance which displaces the pleasures of smoking with a larger than life flaunting of a socially disgraceful self, and the wicked pleasures of self-entertainment. The

American nicotine barons were already denying and covering up the health effects of smoking. In the advertisement Thring flaunts his stage persona, his size, his gestures and eye rolls, his lightness on his feet, almost every element an irony given the association of the cigarettes with showgirl driven glamour. As Kane put it, the fetishised commodity tobacco is generously expanded into 'a problematic object.'

Thring was a delight in himself. I agree, let's not devalue the pleasure his performances brought. We are in the presence of sublime histrionics in which smoking is (never) merely a prop.

Histrionics has other senses than either dramatic exaggeration or psychological pathology. It can also be used to refer more neutrally and generally to conventions of performance and figures of speech. Camp has its own similar problematics. In Isherwood's 1954 novel *The World in the Evening* he employs the distinction between high and low camp. He has one of the characters arguing that camp in its 'High' version is based in the seriousness of artifice: 'You're not making fun of it; you are making fun out of it.' Plainness, the character says, makes elegance necessary. I would push this further. Plainness of design can also be seen on occasion as a form of sophistication – a carefully designed simplicity of surface.

It is this I think which explains the pleasures of my teapot. You may recall I referred in my first reference to the teapot to it having a backward flounce that registers other more ornate times. Its handle that hails earlier times points to the artificiality of the simplicity otherwise found in the teapot's design. Sophistication is founded on figurative conceit. High camp values the complexity involved in producing elegance. Low camp popularises it in Isherwood's character's

192

terms as 'a swishy little boy with peroxided hair …
pretending to be Marlene Dietrich.' My teapot takes
it both ways.

The teapot was a departing gift from
colleagues in the Faculty of Humanities and Social
Sciences at the University of Technology, Sydney,
in 1998. Liz had her hand in buying it. I had been
appointed there in 1985 to teach communication
units to students in other faculties. Over the next
two years I shifted further into Textual Studies
and Cultural Studies. Graham Williams made
valiant attempts to recruit me to teach in the
writing major which I resisted except for two or
three semesters in postgraduate classes. Teaching
at UTS was hard work, but often a joy and in 1992
I received an Excellence in Teaching Award. The
students were smart, challenging and mostly
highly engaged.

Liz was Dean at the time I left UTS. By then I
was a Head of Department, somewhat taken aback
as an active unionist to find myself managing
staff redundancy packages. Liz was on leave when
I decided to apply for one myself. She said later
she would not have approved it. The night of my
farewell in the Concourse Café at the bottom of
the UTS tower Sydney had a major deluge. Streets
were flooded and trees came down. The events
were unrelated. Washed out, but not quite washed
up, I wandered off into the night. Given the rain, I
probably went home.

Some nights are lost forever. It can be hard to
see in the dark.

Hindsight says for all the opportunities UTS
had afforded me, and there were many, it was
right for me to move on. Federal cuts to education
had squeezed teaching methods like seminar
classes in favour of cheaper, more economically
efficient mass lectures, and course offerings were

steadily squeezed. Managerialism had trumped educational priorities and corroded collegial co-operation amongst academics. I was at odds with this, preferring the more personal engagement with students and ideas and the motivational excitement produced in interactive, smaller classes. I was not anti the lecture form in itself, just aware of what it could and couldn't do well. My own sense of what I could do well in those circumstances had faltered, even as what I did in community-based HIV health promotion was increasingly valued and felt more rewarding. Though funding was just as much an issue in that sector, it was work of a different kind. What the two fields had in common was analytically informed social practice. UTS had prepared me well for this, as had more than a decade of deep immersion in lived gay cultures.

In 1999 I went to Waikiki for ten days. I walked the beaches and watched David Fincher's *Fight Club* on a hot, humid afternoon. The air conditioning had collapsed, and the audience dripped with sweat. The film kept me there. It felt strangely salutary. On my way back to my hotel about midnight the following night, a Saturday, a woman stopped me in the street and asked if I wanted a girl. Taken by surprise, I paused then said thank you, but no. She immediately shot back with why not? I'm gay, I said. So what she said, I have a strap-on. We laughed uproariously and after a bit more banter went our separate ways.

A dilettantish interest in fashion re-started for me on that trip to Europe with Leigh at the end of 1987. We spent Christmas that year at Richard Dyer's in Birmingham. Leigh wore a full-length *faux* fur coat to midnight mass with Richard and his mother and another friend. I didn't go. They came back laughing as they shook the snow from their coats. I check my memory of this event in an email.

194

Leigh writes back dryly, 'there are many versions of this anecdote.' He returned to Sydney and stayed in the house that I shared with Kevin.

Late one night in January 1988, in the London Apprentice, then a gay pub in Shoreditch, I met a man in carefully razored 'torn' jeans, fashion punk. We went back to his flat in Dalston, a mile down the road from where I was staying with Virginia in Stoke Newington. Days after we met, he took me to Paul Smith's in Covent Garden and Vivienne Westwood's bare concrete outlet. I could afford nothing. Later still, I borrowed his Comme des Garçons suit for a day to meet family. Sometime around then, we watched *Brief Encounter* together – me for the first time, and then Hitchcock's *Stranger on a Train* (1951). I lost his house keys. He was not impressed.

That first night in Dalston wasn't just any night. We woke in the morning to the radio broadcasting events at the Australian Bicentennial. More than 40,000 people were marching through Sydney streets in support of Aboriginal land rights.

Twelve years later in 2000, well over 200,000 people crossed the Sydney Harbour Bridge in support of Aboriginal Reconciliation. I was one of them. The gaps in the road gave me vertigo. More than half a million marched Australia wide. Australia was inhabited for more than 50,000 years before British colonisation in 1788. Or so we thought. Now it looks more like 65,000. As Megan Davis and Marcia Langton point out, questions of constitutional recognition and a treaty are complicated. Some would argue for practical action rather than grand legal gestures. Others would make the case for both. It is time when asked that we march again with the First Peoples of this country.

After returning to Sydney from London in mid 1988, I watched *Brief Encounter* again with

Chrissie several times over the years, along with *The Lavender Hill Mob*, the BBC le Carré series, and other favourites. It was from her I began to learn about jazz and improvisation. Chrissie died in 2015.

I look across now to the small Japanese vase she gave me as a keepsake. It sits on top of the microwave, safely blue-tacked to avoid breakage. She would approve of that. In my mind, I see her riding her bike down Glebe Point Road, and the camellias she grew in her Erskineville backyard. I think of the annual Oscars night, and other nights listening to jazz at Round Midnight in Kings Cross, the Christmas Days we spent together in my flat in Darlinghurst.

The objects in the china cabinet are not a collection. Nor am I a collector. They are an accumulation of domestic items, gifts over time. Friends knew my tastes, and I see in hindsight how they helped form, develop and encourage them. Writing about them shares aspects of collecting as discussed by art historian Michael Camille: it is 'an active, productive and shaping stimulation of all the senses.' My pleasures are recuperative. I choose to share some of the objects through private display in my small lounge room and as a conceit in this more public writing in a celebration of the generosity of friendship and in one way or another, of other, only sometimes shared, intellectual interests. They are memorabilia. So too are the books I have read.

These are affective matters, partially constituting what I feel as I run the cloth around the body of the teapot experiencing its elliptical shape as I go and hearing the voices of time in the present. One does not have to be either a collector or a connoisseur to know these pleasures. The presence and arrangement of the objects stages them. Their care reignites delight and replays connection. As does writing about them.

I move forward.

Ian MacNeill wrote:

> This is Amelia Earhart
> I'm coming in.

I am polishing a candelabra that holds three candles. It is a new purchase, possibly a mid-twentieth century reproduction of a Georgian design from the late eighteenth century. I bought it by fluke from a St Vincent de Paul opportunity shop in Johnston St., Collingwood, for eight dollars, a gift to myself. Some might think of it as a bit of tat. I had been watering Leigh and Winston's garden while they were away. It had taken me longer to get there than I had allowed, and by then I was at risk of running late to visit David Clement in East Brunswick at his and Marian's house, a bus and a tram away. As I passed the Vinnies op shop, I saw the candelabra in the window. It caught my eye. I liked the look of it but scurried on before suddenly stopping. Buy it now, I thought. You like it, and it won't be there for long. Buggar the money. As Ross Duffin put it in inimitable style, 'consumerism is the rest of the op shop.' I turned and went back. The price was a clincher. I picked it up. It was tarnished, heavier than I thought it would be, but also sinuous: loose-limbed, graceful.

I reached David and Marian's pretty well on time. David and I re-discovered a mutual interest in Miles Davis and John Coltrane. David knows his jazz, much, much better than I do, and still has the vinyl. We sat and talked, all the while listening to Cannonball Adderley's 1958 album 'Somethin' Else'. Miles Davis features on the title track.

David died in July 2020. His death notice in the *Age* referred to a career dedicated to 'supporting workers' rights and the labour movement'. He delighted 'in travel and adventure, good food, great music, fine art and cinema. He described himself as an eternal optimist and lived his life accordingly'.

The candelabra is beginning to shine. In the process of constantly handling and turning it, I start to appreciate its intricacies. One candle cup sits at the top of a central stem. Each of the other two candle cups sit at either end of what I believe are called scrolling arms or branches. These are curved and ridged. The arms begin a third of the way down the stem. They emerge from a wide-ringed junction. Each is like an elongated swollen S laying on its side. They curve out, one to the left and one to the right so the last third of the stem is between them, rising higher. It rises up from a circular base which itself has three layers and narrows towards its top. The stem, however, widens as it rises. The middle layer of the base is ornamented. The stem is mostly plain, except where the branches emerge from the junction just over halfway up, just below the middle ornamented junction on which sits the central candle-hold.

Over the weekend, between the purchase and the polishing, I discuss this design at different times with Marshall Feldman and Cahal Fairfield. Multiple terms are used as each considers it – Georgian, Rococo and more tentatively, Gothic and Nouveau. Between us we know enough to be cautious, though each would agree the design is one thing and the year of production another. We pool bits of half-remembered expertise and bounce off each other's remarks. We are dealing with retro, not an original antique, the re-fashioning of goods. Cahal remarks on the gaps between monarchic periodisations like 'Georgian' and the emergence of design styles with their own name or characteristics. Later I speak with Leigh who thinks the resurgence in Georgian design is a reaction against modernism and post-war American culture, style and success.

One learns there are quite different tastes and traditions. Recognising them and how they work is something else, as is living with their disparities.

As I polish the candelabra, it becomes clear that what I thought was tarnished if not damaged

electroplated nickel silver (EPNS) is entirely intact.
I am as much cleaning as polishing. I turn the
candelabra over to see whether there are markings
on the bottom. I discover that the base has what
seems to be a plain cardboard bottom that likely
covers a hollow. It also appears likely there was
a felt covering that has come away. There is no
obvious way to remove what remains without
damaging it, at least not if I do it. I think it is
possible there are markings inside. Why would I
want to know that? It might confirm which business
produced it. I go on cleaning and polishing and
realise I have uncovered tiny markings on the edge
of the base. I cannot read them. One of the words is
in a frame suggestive of a manufacturer's mark.

I recall I have a magnifying glass that I bought
at a garage sale up the street several years ago. An
old man had lived there alone. I would say hello
in passing. I often saw him out walking. He died,
and the family was preparing the house for sale.
I fossick in the room I once called my study until
it became so full of books and boxes after my
retirement in 2010 that it became a storage space. I
find the magnifying glass. Hoarding has its upsides.
It is still in its original box which also contains
the purchase receipt from OPSM. The magnifier
came with a stand. It was bought in Collins St.,
Melbourne, in 1985. I cannot read the month.

The tiny writing on the edge of the base of the
candelabra reads Silver Plated Withe of England.
Or does it? Even magnified, it is possible I am
misreading Ianthe as Withe. Ianthe is all over eBay
and more specialist sites. I go on polishing and
discover that inside each of the candle cups is a
number, C34. On the opposite side of the right and left
candle-holds is the number 4 and of the centre hold
what might be a 1. It is getting late and I am becoming
unsure whether I myself am inside Dan Brown's *The*

Da Vinci Code (2003) or Umberto Eco's *The Name of the Rose* (1980, tr. 1983). Both are mysteries, and both immerse the reader in arcane knowledge. I suspect silver plating is trying to pass itself off as sterling silver, or more likely it requires I consult with an antiques dealer who knows their stuff.

The photo online of the Ianthe candelabra looks almost identical to mine. There is one difference. The Ianthe candle-cups online have ornamented flat caps with a hole for the candle. These would sit on and into the hold and fix the candles in place. Mine is missing the caps. My pleasure in the candelabra remains.

After photographing it and expanding the photo, Matt says the word is Ianthe. Graham and Dino come over for a weeknight dinner, probably my standby fare, an entree of briefly steamed asparagus quickly fried in garlic and pepper then topped with parmesan, followed by ravioli in a tomato sauce with a salad. Discussion of the candelabra recurs. Dino also says the brand is Ianthe. We discuss the fact that the word has a box around it, and that part of the problem is that the downward stroke on the right side of the 'n' in the middle of the name also functions as the upright of the 't'. Our disruption is graphic. Graham surprises Dino and I by saying the box is called a *cartouche*. I had thought of it as merely a line framing a brand. I ask him how he knows this. He learned it as a long-ago student enrolled in Egyptian history. Royal hieroglyphs were encircled with a mostly oval line. French soldiers in Egypt as part of Napoleon Bonaparte's defence of France's trade thought it resembled a bullet cartridge, hence cartouche. The ancient Egyptians called it a shenu.

We have ice cream with berries for dessert. Spoons clink on everyday bowls, white porcelain with thick and thin blue rings just under the rim.

V

Made in China. My friends leave soon after. I see them off at the gate where the grevillea flowers before returning inside, quietly satisfied. Ianthe it is. I will see them again soon enough.

I put the candelabra on top of the heater. There is no more room in the cabinet.

Michael Hurley has an honorary appointment as an Adjunct Associate Professor at the Australian Research Centre in Sex, Health and Society, La Trobe University, Melbourne, where he worked as an HIV social researcher, 2001–2010. He was an Australia Council Writer in the Community at the AIDS Council of NSW in 1995 and Researcher in Residence at the Australian Federation of AIDS Organisations, 1999–2000. From 1985–1998 he taught textual and cultural studies at the University of Technology, Sydney.

Michael lives in Melbourne with his IKEA china cabinet and a good heater.

Acknowledgements

I wrote the first drafts of this book in Melbourne, Berlin and London in 2016–17. I read parts of those early drafts out loud in Melbourne to Matt Bolden, Gary Dew, Ross Duffin, Cahal Fairfield and Dino Hodge. Mitch Cleary and I discussed teacups and Art Deco china, and Rose Flynn and I spoke of photos of Dusty Springfield. Kevin Mead and I had discussions about china, China and china cabinets that made me think about parlours. I spoke with Marian Pitts about what I was doing, and she informed me on matters to do with the pits and potteries that constitute Stoke-on-Trent in England. Every bit helped.

Marshall Feldman in Los Angeles read progressive drafts along the way for which I am thankful. His interest, support and knowledge kept me going. Sometimes I thought he understood what it was I was doing better than I did. Graham Willett asked the right questions at the right times about particular sections, as he does, and I took advantage of this to write more and differently. By then I was in Berlin. Graham was moving around Europe. We talked, emailed and messaged. I spoke with Gary about various matters over WhatsApp. In London, Lynne Segal read, commented, suggested, encouraged, read again, loaned books and I learned, took heart and example, and enjoyed her garden and hospitality. I knew by then I had a book on my hands. It was a lovely summer. Ford Hickson and I discussed Charles Hawtrey, Kenneth Williams and *Carry On* movies. Will Nutland and I talked our projects over coffee in Shoreditch Grind. In the last days of my stay in London in July–August 2017, Julie Bishop read the fullest draft at that point. She got it. That mattered.

Once I was back in Melbourne, Cahal expanded as needed what little I knew of *chinoiserie* in the late

Regency period. I was almost there. Marian Pitts read, re-read, made suggestions and read again. We drank coffee in Tin Pot, Melbourne coffee. Dino read it, commented and strengthened my understanding of various matters. Graham too read it yet again and saved me from some embarrassing errors as did Kirsty Machon. Both Kirsty and Pam Brown gave further good advice of various kinds. From mid 2018 into 2019 Tim Herbert read and reread the manuscript, each time making a series of suggestions. I rewrote and the book changed markedly. Kirsty copy edited it and Leigh Raymond then made publication happen.

I checked the accuracy of what I said about many of the people mentioned in the book with them, where I thought it was needed, and they also offered corrections and suggestions.

I am very grateful to all.

Much appreciation and final thanks go to the Australian Lesbian and Gay Archives who agreed to put their name on the book as publisher, just as they had done alongside Allen and Unwin in 1996 with *A Guide to Gay and Lesbian Writing in Australia*.

While I searched various literatures on the objects, events, places and people referred to in this book, I have written about them with I hope a relatively light hand, quoting and sometimes commenting on them as I go. The book is informed by the work of others – see the Sources section following – but what I do with that work in my writing is my responsibility.

Sources

Note: I have used a simplified citation system. Direct quotes in the main text of a sentence or more are given page numbers from within the relevant book or article in the order I quote them. For quotes from films and tv series I refer only to the director, the year of release and the title. For quotes from online newspaper and magazine articles I have cited the articles but omitted web addresses easily found with a Google search using key words.

Adair, J. (2010) 'One must be ruthless in the cause of Beauty': Beverley Nichols's and John Fowler's Queer Domesticity.' *Visual Culture and Gender*, 5.

Albury, K. (2002) *Yes means yes: getting explicit about heterosex*. St Leonards, NSW: Allen & Unwin.

Altman, D. and Symons, J. (2016) *Queer wars: The new global polarization over gay rights*. Cambridge, UK: Polity Press, p 5.

Altman, D. (1971) *Homosexual. Oppression and Liberation*. San Francisco: Gay Sunshine Press, p 186.

Barthes, R. (1992) *Incidents*. Berkeley: University of California Press, p 14.

Barthes, R. (1981) Preface. In Camus, R. *Tricks. 25 Encounters*. New York: St Martin's Press, pp vii, viii.

Barthes, R. (1991) *The Grain of the Voice: Interviews, 1962–1980*. Berkeley: University of California Press.

Barthes, R. (1977) *Roland Barthes by Roland Barthes*. London: MacMillan, p 117.

Barthes, R. [1957, tr 1972] (2000) *Mythologies*. London: Vintage Books, p 56.

Bartlett, K. (2014) *Dusty: An Intimate Portrait of a Musical Legend*. London: Robson Press,, p 2.

Bartlett, N. quoted in Sinfield, A. (1996) 'The Moment of Submission: Neil Bartlett in Conversation.' *Modern Drama*, 39, p 218.

Bartlett, N. (1988) *Who was that Man? A Present for Mr Oscar Wilde*. London: Serpent's Tail, p 46.

Bashford, K., Jones, C., Kerans, P., Knight, L., Moulstone, J., and Moulstone, W. (Eds.) (1991) *Pink Ink. An anthology of Australian lesbian and gay writers*. Sydney: Jasper Laybutt/Wicked Women Publications.

Baudelaire, C. (1981) *Baudelaire: Selected Writings on Art and Artists*. Cambridge, UK: Cambridge University Press, p 421.

Beachy, R. (2015) *Gay Berlin. Birthplace of a modern identity*. New York: Vintage.

Benfey, C. (1998). https://www.nytimes.com/1998/02/22/magazine/flashback.html

Benjamin, W. (2002) *The Arcades Project*. Cambridge, Massachusetts: Belknap, p 447.

Benjamin, W. [1935] (1968). 'The Work of Art in the Age of Mechanical Reproduction.' In Arendt, H. (1992) (Ed.) *Illuminations.Walter Benjamin*. London: Fontana.

Bennett, A. (2009) *A Life Like Other People's*. London: Faber and Faber.

Blais, M. (1979) 'Tennessee in the Tropics.' *Washington Post* 4 April.

Bourdieu, P. (1984) *Distinction. A social critique of the judgement of taste*. Cambridge, Massachusetts, USA: Harvard University Press.

Bowker, G. (2003) *Inside George Orwell*. London: Palgrave Macmillan.

Bradshaw, P. (2013) 'The Servant: a 60s masterwork that hides its homosexuality in the shadows'. *Guardian* 27 March.

Brendon, P. (2003) 'The Saint of Common Decency'. *Guardian* 7 June.

Brohan Museum (2017), booklet, 'Germany against France. The Struggle over Style, 1900–1930.' Berlin: Brohan Museum.

Brown, P. (2015) 'West End Blues' in *Missing Up*. Vagabond Press: Sydney, pp 11–15.

Brown, P. (1996) 'Ol' Shallow Throat.' In Berry C. and Jagose, A. (Eds.) *Australia Queer* edition. *Meanjin* 1, pp 170–171.

Burnheim, J. (2011) *To Reason Why: From religion to philosophy and beyond*. Sydney: Darlington Press.

Calder, B. (2016) *Pink Ink. The Golden Era for Gay and Lesbian Magazines*. Newcastle upon Tyne: Cambridge Scholars Publishing.

Calvet, L-J. (1995) *Roland Barthes. A biography*. Bloomington: Indiana University Press, pp x, 177, 136, 50.

Camille, M. (2001) Introduction. In Camille, M. and Rifkin, A. (2001) (Eds.), *Other Objects of Desire: Collectors and Collecting Queerly*. Oxford, England: Blackwell.

Carmody, M. (2015) *Sex, Ethics and Young People*. New York: Palgrave Macmillan.

Carmody, M. (2009) *Sex & ethics: young people and ethical sex*. South Yarra, Vic.: Palgrave Macmillan.

Chambers. R. (1999) *Loiterature*. Lincoln, Nebraska: University of Nebraska Press, pp 252, 254, 255–256, 260–262.

Chervenka, M. (nd) 'Clarice Cliff Pottery.' www.realorrepro.com/article/Clarice-Cliff--Pottery

Clarke, B. (2007) *Orwell in Context. Communities, myths, values.* London: Palgrave MacMillan, pp 93–97.

Connolly, C. [1938] (2008) *Enemies of Promise.* Chicago: University of Chicago Press, p 47.

Cook, M. (2014) *Queer Domesticities. Homosexuality and Home Life in Twentieth-Century London.* London: Palgrave MacMillan, pp 27, 85.

Core, P. (1999) 'Camp: The Lie That Tells the Truth.' In Cleto, F. (Ed.) *Camp: Queer Aesthetics and the Performing Subject: A Reader.* Ann Arbor: University of Michigan Press, p 83.

Dalby, S. (1999) 'Pot Luck for Cliff Lovers.' *Guardian* 9 January.

Davis, M. and Langton, M. (2016) *It's Our Country. Indigenous arguments for meaningful constitutional recognition and reform.* Melbourne: Melbourne University Press.

Day, R. (1960). Dir. *Two-Way Stretch*, UK.

Debord, G. [1967] (1995) *The Society of the Spectacle.* New York: Zone Books, p 12.

Dermody, S. and Jacka, E. (1987–88) *The Screening of Australia.* Sydney: Currency Press.

Dermody, S. and Jacka, E. (Eds.) (1988) *The Imaginary Industry. Australian film in the late '80s.* North Ryde: Australian Film, Television and Radio School.

Dessaix, R. (1993) *Australian Gay and Lesbian writing: An anthology.* Melbourne: Oxford University Press.

Docker, J. (1984) *In a Critical Condition. Reading Australian literature.* Ringwood: Penguin.

Dollimore, J. (1991) *Sexual Dissidence.* New York: Oxford University Press, p 33.

Down, I., Bradley, J., Ellard, J., Brown, G., Grulich, A., Prestage, G. (2010). *Experiences of HIV: The Seroconversion Study Annual Report 2010.* Monograph. Sydney: The Kirby Institute, University of New South Wales.

Drake, A. (2006) *The Beautiful Fall. Fashion, genius and beautiful excess in 1970s Paris.* London: Bloomsbury.

Dyer, R. [1993] (2015) *Brief Encounter.* London: Bloomsbury Publishing, pp 13, 14 .

Dyer, R. (1997) *White.* London and New York: Routledge, p 45.

Dyer, R. (1986) *Heavenly Bodies. Film Stars and Society.* New York: St Martin's Press.

Dyer, R. (1977) *Gays and Film.* London: British Film Institute.

Edie, J.M. (1964) *The Primacy of Perception: And Other Essays on Phenomenological Psychology, the Philosophy of Art, History and Politics.* Northwestern University Press, Evanston, Illinois, p 5.

Ellmann, R. (1988) *Oscar Wilde.* London: Penguin, p 43.

Eshun, E. (2016) 'The Subversive Power of the Black Dandy.' *Guardian*, 5 July.

Farson, D. (1993) 'Obituary. Francis Bacon.' *Independent*, 24 April.

Feldman, G.D. (1993) *The Great Disorder: Politics, economics, and society in the German inflation, 1914–1924*. New York: Oxford University Press.

Fisher, H. (2015) 'The Queen of Androgyny – Marlene Dietrich.' www.barnebys.co.uk

Forbes, J. (2001) 'Watching the Treasurer' in *New and Selected Poems*. Sydney: Angus and Robertson, p 65.

Foucault, M. (1985) *The Use of Pleasure*. New York: Pantheon, p 8.

Frears, S. (1995) Dir. *My Beautiful Laundrette*. UK.

Freney, D. (1991) *A Map of Days. Life on the Left*. Melbourne: William Heinemann.

Fryer, J. (1977) *Isherwood: A Biography*. Garden City, NY: Doubleday & Company.

Glover, D. (2017) 'The Erotics of Restraint or the Angel in the Novel: A note on Jane Austen's *Mansfield Park*', March 1, http://brooklynrail.org/2017/03/fiction/Erotics-of-Restraint

Goldie, T. (2008) *QueerSexLife. Autobiographical notes on sexuality, gender and identity*. Vancouver: Arsenal Pulp Press.

Grant, C. (2017) 'Familiar Stranger by Stuart Hall review – from Jamaica to the New Left and Thatcherism.' *Guardian*, 31 March.

Griffin, L, Meisel, L. and Meisel, S. (1988) *Clarice Cliff. The Bizarre Affair*. London: Thames and Hudson.

Guardian (2012) 'From the Observer archive, 6 March 1960: Marlene Dietrich's wardrobe secrets.' 4 March.

Haggarty, G. and Zimmerman, B. (2000) *The Encyclopaedia of Lesbian and Gay Histories and Cultures*, Vol. 2. London and New York: Garland. See the entry 'Flowers and Birds'.

Hall, S, (2017). *Selected Political Writings: The great moving right show and other essays*. London: Lawrence and Wishart.

Hall, S., with Schwarz, B. (2017). *Familiar Stranger. A Life Between Two Islands.* Durham: Duke University Press, p 271.

Hall, S. (1988) *The Hard Road to Renewal*. London and New York: Verso, pp 193–94.

Halperin, D. and Hoppe, T. (Eds.) (2017) *The War on Sex*. Durham/London: Duke University Press.

Halperin, D. (2012) *How to be Gay*. Cambridge USA: Harvard University Press, pp 362, 363, 366.

Hamilton, J. (2016) *Just around Midnight. Rock and Roll and the Racial Imagination*. Massachusetts: Harvard University Press, p 193.

Harper, S. and Porter, V. (2003) *British Cinema of the 1950s: The Decline of Deference*. Oxford: Oxford University Press.

Harris, G.. and Witte, J. (nd) 'The First Mardi Gras: 40 years on.' www.kxacf.org.au

Hawkins, G. (2013) 'Taste.' In Bennett, T., Grossberg, L. and Morris, M., (Eds.) *New Keywords: A Revised Vocabulary of Culture and Society*. Melbourne: Wiley-Blackwell.

Hawtrey, C. http://www.astabgay.com/KingsOfCamp/ CharlesHawtrey.htm

Hodge, D. (2014) *Don Dunstan, Intimacy and Liberty. A political biography*. Adelaide: Wakefield Press, pp 298, 269, 268, 6–7.

Hoppe, T. (2018) *Punishing Disease. HIV and the Criminalization of Sickness*. Oakland: University of California Press.

Hughes, J. (2006) book review of *Go! Melbourne. Age*, 21 January.

Hughes, R. (1980) *The Shock of the New: Art and the century of change*. London: BBC, p 12.

Hurley M. (2015) 'In memoriam: Alan Brotherton (1963–2015)'. *HIV Australia*, 13/2, April.

Hurley, M. (2015) 'We're not all Straight in the Garden State'. In Blackburn, S. (ed.), *Breaking Out. Memories of Melbourne in the 1970s*. Sydney: Hale and Iremonger.

Hurley, M. (2014) 'We were Rocking and Reeling.' In Rule, J. (Ed.) *Through Our Eyes. Thirty years of people living with HIV responding to the HIV and AIDS epidemics in Australia*. Sydney: NAPWHA.

Hurley, M. (2011) 'When HIV is Endemic amongst Gay Men.' In Smaal, Y. and Willett, G. (Eds.) *Out Here. Gay and Lesbian Perspectives VI*. Melbourne: Monash University Press.

Hurley, M. (2011) 'Aspects of Gay and Lesbian Life in Seventies Melbourne.' *The Latrobe Journal*. 87 May.

Hurley, M. (2010) VIH, santé sexuelle et cultures gaies contemporaines. In Olivier Jablonski, Jean-Yves Le Talec, Georges Sidéris (eds), Sante Gaie. Paris: L'harmattan – Editions Pepper.

Hurley, M. and Prestage, G. (2009) 'Intensive sex partying amongst gay men in Sydney.' *Culture Health & Sexuality*, 11 (6).

Hurley, M (2007) 'Who's on Whose Margins?' In M. Pitts & A. Smith (Eds.), *Researching the Margins. Strategies for Ethical and Rigorous Research with Marginalised Communities*. London: Palgrave Macmillan.

Hurley, M. (2005) 'Contemporary Gay Cultures in Australia.'
In Hawkes, G. and Scott, J. (Eds.) *Perspectives in Human
Sexuality*. Melbourne: Oxford University Press.

Hurley, M. (2005) *Culture and Community: Researching gay and
lesbian lives 1990–2005*. PhD (University of Technology,
Sydney).

Hurley, M. (2003) *Then and Now. Gay men and HIV*. Monograph
Number 46. Melbourne: Australian Research Centre in
Sex, Health and Society, La Trobe University.

Hurley, M. (2002) (Ed.) *Cultures of Care and Safe Sex amongst
HIV Positive Australians. Papers from the HIV Futures
I and II surveys and interviews*. Melbourne: Australian
Research Centre in Sex, Health and Society, La Trobe
University.

Hurley, M (2002) 'A Critical Reflection.' In Aitken, G. (Ed) *The
Penguin Book of Australian Gay Writing*, Melbourne:
Penguin.

Hurley, M. (2001) 'A Shopping Bag from Harrods.' In Kellehear,
A. (Ed) *Grief. Twenty Five Australians tell it like it is*.
Melbourne: Rivoli.

Hurley, M. (2001) 'Sydney.' In Johnston, C. and van Ryke, P.
(Eds) *Queer City. Gay and lesbian politics in Sydney*,
Annandale, NSW: Pluto Press.

Hurley, M. (1999) 'A Tale of Three Daddies.' Unpublished
panel presentation. Australian Homosexual Histories 2
conference, University of Melbourne, November.

Hurley, M. (1997) 'Introduction.' In Drinnan, N., and Luker, T.,
(Eds) *Fruit Salad. A compote of contemporary gay and
lesbian writing*, Sydney: Sydney Gay and Lesbian Mardi
Gras.

Hurley, M. and Hutchinson J. (1995) 'Two Timing, A
Retrospective.' In Dunne, G., compiler, *Collected Papers,
Second National QueerLit Conference*, Sydney.

Hurley, M. (1995) 'T.S. Eliot was a Bank Clerk.' In Blazey, P.,
Dawson, V. and Herbert, T. (Eds.) *Love Cries*. Sydney:
Harper/Collins.

Hurley, M. (1995) 'FF: A Film and a Funeral.' In North, G, and
McClean, S., (Eds.) *Divertika*. Sydney: City Media.

Hurley, M. (1993) 'Erotic Writing.' In Dunne G., compiler, *A Cold
Collation, Papers from the Inaugural QueerLit Conference*,
Sydney.

Hurley, M. (1992) 'AIDS Narratives, Gay Sex and the Hygienics of
Innocence.' *Southern Review*, July.

Hurley, M. (1992) 'Writing, The Body Positive.' *Meanjin* 1(1)
Autumn.

Hurley, M. (1991) 'Introduction: Writing, the body positive.' In
Bashford, K., Halliday, M.,

Jones, C., Kerans, P., Knight, L., Moulstone, J., and Moulstone, W. (Eds.) (1991) *Pink Ink. An anthology of Australian lesbian and gay writers*. Sydney: Jasper Laybutt/Wicked Women Publications.

Hurley, M. and Hutchinson, J. (1991) *Two Timing. Sex, writing and the writing of sex*. Sydney: Local Consumption Publications.

Hurley, M. (1990) 'Homosexualities: Fiction, reading and moral training.' In Threadgold, T., and. Cranny-Francis, A., (Eds.) *Feminine, Masculine and Representation*. Sydney: Allen & Unwin.

Hurley, M. (1984) *Realism Resuscitated: The Novels of Elizabeth Harrower and Jessica Anderson*. (Master of Letters, University of New England, Armidale, NSW).

Hurley, M. (1983) 'Sweet Bird of Youth. Tennessee Williams 1911–1983.' *Outrage* 1, April.

Hurley, M. and Johnston, C. (1976). 'Campfires of the Resistance: Theory and Practice for the Liberation of Male Homosexuals.' In *Papers and Proceedings, First National Homosexual Conference, Melbourne, 16–17 August,1975*. Melbourne: Homosexual Conference Collective.

Irvin, J. (1979). Dir. seven part miniseries, *Tinker Taylor Soldier Spy*. BBC TV.

Isherwood, C. (1976) *Christopher and His Kind*. New York: Farrar, Straus and Giroux.

Isherwood, C. (1954) *The World in the Evening*. London: Methuen, p 125.

Isherwood, C. (1939) *Goodbye to Berlin*. London: Hogarth Press.

Isherwood, C. (1935) *Mr Norris Changes Trains*. London: Hogarth Press.

Jennings, R. (2007) *Tomboys and Bachelor Girls. A Lesbian History of Postwar Britain*. Manchester: Manchester University Press.

Johnson, L. (1993) 'Davey, John Andrew (Jack) (1907–1959).' *Australian Dictionary of Biography*. http://adb.anu.edu.au/biography/davey-john-andrew-jack-9905

Johnston, C. (1999). *A Sydney Gaze: The making of gay liberation*. Darlinghurst, NSW: Schiltron.

Jones, O. (1868) *The Grammar of Ornament*. London: Bernard Quaritch.

Julien, I (1989) Dir. *Looking for Langston*. UK.

Julien, I. and Mercer, K. (1988) 'Introduction – De Margin and De Centre.' *Screen* 29: 4.

Keating, P. http://www.keating.org.au/shop/item/for-the-new-australia---11-november-1996

Kehr, D. (2012) 'That Well-lighted Agent of Desire.' *New York Times*, 3 March.

Keneally, T. (1968) *Three Cheers for the Paraclete*. Sydney: Angus and Robertson.

Kennison, R. (2002) 'Clothes Make the (Wo)man.' *Journal of Lesbian Studies*, 6:2.

Knight, L. (2005) *Clarice Cliff*. London: Bloomsbury

Krauss, R. (1986) *The Originality of the Avant-Garde and Other Modernist Myths*. Cambridge, Massachusetts, and London: MIT Press.

Kureishi, H. (1986) *My Beautiful Laundrette and The Rainbow Sign*. London: Faber and Faber, pp 38, 35.

Lake, R. (2015) 'Alan Brotherton's HIV diagnosis spurred 30 years of effective advocacy'. *Sydney Morning Herald*, August 7.

Lean, D. (1945) Dir. *Brief Encounter*. UK.

Lehmann, J. (1976) *In the Purely Pagan Sense*. London: Blond and Briggs. Chs. viii–xi.

Livermore, R. (2004) *Reg Livermore. Chapters and Chances*. Prahran: Hardie &Grant, p 112.

Machon, K. (1996) *Immortalities*. Sydney: Blackwattle Press

MacNeill, I. (1989) 'Amelia Earhart' in *TV Tricks and Other Poems*. Sydney: Blackwattle Press, p 46.

Madden, E. (2000) 'Flowers and Birds', in Haggarty, G. and Zimmerman, B. (2000) *The Encyclopaedia of Lesbian and Gay Histories and Cultures*, Vol. 2. London and New York: Garland.

McDiarmid, D. (1997) 'A Short History of Facial Hair.' In Matthews, J. (Ed.) *Sex in Public: Australian Sexual Cultures*. Sydney: Allen & Unwin, p 92. The chapter was originally a talk given at the Positive Living Centre, Melbourne in 1993.

McDiarmid, D. (1992) *Toxic Queen*. Darlington, Sydney, NSW.

McGuiness, M. (2020) 'Babylon Berlin captures the murky glamour of the late Weimar period.' *Financial Times*, March 18.

McKemmish, J. (1985) *A Gap in the Records*, Melbourne: Sybylla Co-operative Press, p 1.

Menadue, D. (2003) *Positive*. Crows Nest, N.S.W: Allen & Unwin.

Millar, G. (1991) Dir. television film *A Murder of Quality*. ITV, UK.

Miller, D.A. (1992) *Bringing Out Roland Barthes*. Berkeley: University of California Press, pp 16–23, 6–7.

Mitchell, T. (2001) 'Memorializing Dusty Springfield: Millennial Mourning, Whiteness, Fandom, and the Seductive Voice.' *Topia*. Canadian Journal of Cultural Studies 6, pp 95, 85.

Modjeska, D. (1990) *Poppy*. Melbourne: McPhee Gribble.

Modjeska, D. and Pizer, M. (Eds.) (1985) *The Poems of Lesbia Harford*. Sydney:Sirius.

Modjeska, D. (1981) *Exiles at home: Australian women writers, 1925–1945*. Sydney: Angus and Robertson.

Morley, D. and Schwartz, B. (2014) 'Stuart Hall Obituary.' *Guardian*, 10 February.

Morris, M. (2014) 'Introducing Ross Chambers.' *Cultural Studies Review*, 20/1, p 169.

Morris, M. (1992a) Foreword, *Ecstasy and Economics. American Essays for John Forbes*. Sydney: Empress Publishing, pp 10, 18–20.

Morris, M. (1992b) 'Ecstasy and Economics (A Portrait of Paul Keating).' *Discourse*, 14/3 (Summer).

Murphy, P. (nd) 'Building up to Sydney's First Gay and Lesbian Mardi Gras.' www.roughreds.com/rrtwo/murphy.html

Nash, B. (nd) http://www.cabaret-berlin.com/?tag=the-blue-angel

Nestle, J. and Preston, J. (1994) (Eds.) *Sister and Brother. Lesbians and Gay Men Write about their Lives Together*. USA: HarperCollins.

Nestle, J. (1987) *A Restricted Country. Essays and Short Stories*. Ithaca, NY: Firebrand Books, p 100.

No Angel – A Life of Marlene Dietrich, (1996, Doco. Dir. Chris Hunt).

Nutland, W. (2014) 'Why HIV Preventions Meds Should be Available on the. NHS Now.' *New Statesman*. December 1.

Pallotta-Chiarolli, M. (2011) 'Messing up the Couples Cabinet'. In Marsh, V. (Ed.) *Speak now: Australian perspectives on same-sex marriage*. Melbourne: Clouds of Magellan.

Pater, W. (1873) *The Renaissance: studies in art and poetry*. hwww.gutenberg.org/files/2398/2398-h/2398-h.htm

Patterson, J. (2015) '*Brief Encounter*: Is it still relevant at 70?' *Guardian* 2 November.

Pells, R. (2016) 'The controversial moment that led George Michael to publicly acknowledge he was gay.' *Independent* 26 December.

Peppiatt, M. (2016) *Francis Bacon in Your Blood. A memoir*. London: Bloomsbury.

Peterson, R. (2005) *A Place of Sensuous Resort: Buildings of St Kilda and Their People*. St Kilda Historical Society. Ch 16. Online.

Phillips, A, A. (1958) *The Australian Tradition: Studies in colonial culture*. Melbourne: FW Cheshire

Pierpont, CR. (1999) 'Another Country. Baldwin's Flight from America.' *New Yorker* 9 Feb.

Porter, D. (2001) 'Faith'. In *Other Worlds: Poems 1997–2001*. Chippendale, NSW: Picador, p 38.

Postrel, V. (2013) *The Power of Glamour. Longing and the art of visual persuasion*. New York: Simon and Schuster, chapter. 1.

Prestage, G., Duncan, D., Grierson, J., et al., (2015) *Monopoly: A study of gay men's relationships*, Report 2014. Sydney, Australia: The Kirby Institute, The University of New South Wales.

Prestage, G, McCann, P.D, Hurley, M, Down, I, Brown, G. (2010). *Pleasure and Sexual Health. The PASH Study, 2009*. Monograph. Sydney: National Centre in HIV Epidemiology and Clinical Research.

Race, K. (2017) ' "The things one does! The things one believes in!" Commodity Culture, Gay Play and the Thringing of Addiction', 31 August. www.homotectonic.com

Race, K. (2016) 'Thinking with Pleasure: Agency & Experimentation', 20 November. www. homotectonic.com

Reif, R. (1983) 'Antique View; Pottery with an Art Deco Touch.' *New York Times* 24 July.

Rogers, B. (1995) 'Death of the author. Roland Barthes: A Biography by Louis-Jean Calvet.' *Independent* 8 January.

Röntgen, R. (1996) *The Book of Meissen*. Atglen, PA: Schiffer. See also https://en.wikipedia.org/wiki/Bone_china

Ross, L. (2013) *Revolution is for Us: The left and gay liberation in Australia*. Melbourne: Intervention.

Roszak, T. (1969) *The making of a counter culture. Reflections on the technocratic society and its youthful opposition.* New York: Anchor Books.

Rothwell, N. (1986) 'Gay book launch with a difference.' *Weekend Australian*, 6–7 December: 6.

Segal, L. (2013) *Out of Time: The Pleasures and the Perils of Ageing*. London: Verso, p 181.

Segal, L. (1990) *Slow Motion. Changing Masculinities, Changing Men*. London: Virago.

Shklovsky, V. (1965) 'Art as Technique'. In Lemon, L. and Reis, E. (Eds) *Russian Formalist Criticism: Four Essays*. Lincoln USA and London, UK: University of Nebraska Press.

Silvester, C. (1997) 'Never a Normal Man. Daniel Farson.' *Sunday Times* 16 March.

Simonson, R. (2014) 'From "Goodbye to Berlin" to I Am a Camera, A History of Cabaret's Journey to the Stage.' *Playbill* 11 April.

Smith, A. (2005) 'Lonely Garbo's love secret is exposed.' *Observer* 11 September.

Smith, D. (2005) 'Lesbian Novel was "danger to nation." ' *Observer* 2 January.

Sontag, S. (1983) 'Writing Itself: On Roland Barthes', Introduction, in Sontag, S. (Ed.) *Barthes: Selected Writings*. Oxford: Fontana, pp xxvi-xxvii.

Sontag, S. (1966) *Against Interpretation and Other Essays*. New York: Farrar, Straus and Giroux.

Steele, D.R. (nd) 'My Orwell Right or Wrong'. http://www.la-articles.org.uk/orwell.pdf

Sternweiler, A. (2008) *Self-Confidence and Persistence. Two Hundred Years of History*. Berlin: Schwules Museum.

Symons, J. and Altman, D. (2016) 'Queer wars: the best place to start promoting gay rights is at home'. *The Conversation*, 8 March.

Weeks, J. (2017) '50 years of legal gay sex.' *Boyz* 26 July.

White, E. (2012) 'Christopher Isherwood's Liberation.' *Guardian* 1 June.

White, E. (1998) *Proust. A Life*. New York: Penguin Random House, p 46.

Wieland, K. (2011) *Dietrich and Riefenstahl. Hollywood, Berlin and a century in two lives*. New York: Liveright Publishing, 74, 55,

Wilde, O. (1879) *Essays and Lectures*. http://www.gutenberg.org/ebooks/774

Wilde, O. (1889) 'The Decay of Lying' Accessed https://www.sscnet.ucla.edu/comm/steen/cogweb/Abstracts/Wilde_1889.html

Wilde, O. (1895) *The Importance of Being Earnest*. Act 1. Accessed https://www.gutenberg.org/files/844/844-h/844-h.htm

Wilde, O. [1891] (1998) *The Picture of Dorian Gray*. Ontario: Broadview Press, p 116.

Williams, R. (2001) '*Far from the Madding Crowd*'. In Open University (Ed.), *The Nineteenth-Century Novel. A Critical Reader*. London: Psychology Press.

Williams, R. (1977) *Marxism and Literature*. Oxford University Press.

Williams, R. (1961) *The Long Revolution*. London: Chatto and Windus.

Williams, R. (1958) *Culture and Society*. London: Chatto and Windus.

Willett, G. (2000) *Living Out Loud. A History of Gay and Lesbian Activism in Australia*. St Leonards, NSW: Allen & Unwin.

Willett, G. (1999) 'Craig Johnston, A Sydney Gaze: The Making of Gay Liberation'. *Arena*.

Wilson, AN. (2013) 'George Orwell's doublethink.' *Spectator*. October.

Winterson, J. (2017) 'Queer politics has been a force for change.' *Guardian* 27 July.

Wolfe, T. (1966) *The Kandy-Kolored Tangerine-Flake Streamlined Baby*. New York: Farrar, Straus and Giroux.

Woolworths Museum website. www.woolworthsmuseum.co.uk/hg-chinaglass.htm

Wotherspoon, G. (Ed.) (1986) *Being Different*. Hale & Iremonger: Sydney.

Yahp, B., Daly, M. and Falconer, L. (Eds.) (1990) *My Look's Caress: A collection of modern romances*. Sydney: Local Consumption Publications.

Yang, W. (1997) *Friends of Dorothy*. Sydney: Pan MacMillan, p 99.

Zweig, S. (1942) *The World of Yesterday. Memories of a European*. New York: Viking Press.